Human Trafficking and the Feminization of Poverty

Human Trafficking and the Feminization of Poverty

Structural Violence in Cambodia

Yuko Shimazaki

LEXINGTON BOOKS

Lanham • Boulder • New York • London

Published by Lexington Books
An imprint of The Rowman & Littlefield Publishing Group, Inc.
4501 Forbes Boulevard, Suite 200, Lanham, Maryland 20706
www.rowman.com

6 Tinworth Street, London SE11 5AL, United Kingdom

British Library Cataloguing in Publication Information Available

Library of Congress Control Number: 2020944858
ISBN 978-1-7936-3471-9 (cloth)
ISBN 978-1-7936-3473-3 (pbk)
ISBN 978-1-7936-3472-6 (electronic)

To all people who have experienced human trafficking and to the trafficked women and girls who have broken their silence and put their feelings and thoughts into words.

Contents

List of Maps

Map 0.1   Cambodia, Map No. 3860 Rev. 4, January 2004. *Source*: United Nations.

Map 0.2   Southeast Asia, Map No. 4365 Rev. 1, March 2012. *Source*: United Nations.

Preface

Human trafficking is the commercial trade of persons and the crime of buying and selling them as commercial items. In the process of trafficking, persons are exploited through the deprivation of their human rights. Furthermore, they are put in a state of servitude or enslavement. At present, the way human trafficking is committed has become so cleverly complicated and subtle that it makes it much harder than ever to understand the whole picture of the ongoing situation.

In Cambodia, a society which embraces the relationship between subordinates and superiors is well established. Women and girls, situated at the bottom of the hierarchy, are more likely to be victimized by human trafficking than men. Some trafficking victims are taken from the villages of their origin to such neighboring countries as Thailand. Others are, from Thailand acting as one of the main transit places, taken to be sold in the global market of the human trafficking business.

At home in Cambodia, under the initiative of international organizations and NGOs working on the human trafficking issue, the victims of human trafficking and those who are put in a socially marginalized position are now provided with shelter and protection. Some victims have learned vocational skills and knowledge with the help and support of these organizations, and have taken the first step toward achieving their own economic independence after many hardships in their lives. There are several cases where those who were in marginalized positions in society finally achieved their own independence socially and economically. In the process of their achievement, they learned to develop a sense of self-help and gained self-knowledge toward the circumstances they were faced with. When those who are regarded as the vulnerable and the victims of structural violence in Cambodia come to realize the importance of self-awareness and self-direction, and set forth on leading lives of their own, they will have taken the first step toward liberating themselves from the poverty they were trapped in. Yet, if those international organizations and NGOs concerned with the issues only offer temporary and one-sided support to the vulnerable and the victims, it becomes far more difficult for them to achieve their independence, because it takes a long time for them to reach their self-fulfillment after the various economic and social hardships they meet. In reality, there are quite a few cases in which some people left their task half-finished, and in the end, they fell back into the harsh reality of poverty again.

This book would like to answer the questions "Why does human trafficking occur?" "Who are the victims of human trafficking in the context of Cambodia?" and "What makes a person a target of human trafficking?" The author's long-term field research in Cambodia will support the answers. To be more concrete, this book attempts to explain how and why women and girls, situated in a marginalized position at the bottom of the Cambodian social hierarchy, are affected by structural violence in a detailed way. Under the influence of the Cambodian social structure, they become involved in "human trafficking" before they know it. How and why they are involved against their will in the power structure is going to be considered. Several theoretical tools will be given and explained in order to have a broader understanding of human trafficking, so as not to be content just with understanding the example cases of human trafficking incidents in this book.

Some of the trafficked victims in Cambodia learned to look at themselves objectively and to develop a sense of self-awareness and self-direction. Furthermore, they learned to use their own initiative in their own lives. In this phase, they should not be regarded as social victims or the vulnerable any longer, but as individuals who hold out their hands to those who need help and share a sense of solidarity with other needy persons, feel a growing awareness of self-respect and of human dignity within themselves, and have confidence in setting themselves free from the poverty trap. This book attempts to illustrate the process of achieving their economic and social independence and also that of their awareness of self-motivation.

The results collected from the interviews with the trafficked victims and their family members were based on the research conducted during the period 2004–2008. The author spent consecutive periods extending over twelve years from 2004 to 2016 on field research including a follow-up survey to finish this book, first published in Japanese by Akashi Publishing (Akashi Shoten) (Tokyo, 2018) as「人身売買と貧困の女性化-カンボジアにおける構造的暴力-」.

This study employs qualitative research as the main method, as well as relies on earlier research and references, and conducts observations and interviews. All the interviews and pictures were taken by the author in Cambodia. Two types of approaches were organized for data collection: one approach was to rely on referrals to potential new interviewees by others who had been interviewed and the other is that interviewees were selected at random. Interviewees included (1) the victims of human trafficking and their family members; (2) staff members of international organizations and NGOs; (3) administrative chiefs, the village leaders and the members of the neighborhood association, the residents of the same village, and experts familiar with the actual condition of the researched areas.

The author interviewed the victims of trafficking or presumed victims of trafficking in a shelter when they were temporarily accommodated there for protection. Some of the interviewees had already returned to their home villages in which case the author visited them in their home villages to interview them. Conducting this research required strict adherence to professional ethics because the survey of human trafficking requires careful and delicate handling in order to safeguard the privacy and human rights of the interviewees. The author conducted all the interviews in accordance with the *WHO Ethical and Safety Recommendations for Interviewing Trafficked Women*, released by the World Health Organization. In the survey, the highest priority was given to the safety of these trafficked victims, protecting their identities and keeping their names anonymous. The author also tried to minimize the social and emotional risks for them. The author was accompanied on her field research by people who were appropriately selected. The research was carried out in accordance with the ethical guidelines and supplementary requirements produced by the United Nations Inter-Agency Project (UNIAP) with *Human Trafficking Guide to Ethics and Human rights in Counter-Trafficking: Ethical Standards for Counter Trafficking Research and Programming* that specializes in human trafficking in cooperation with UN organizations. All the names and the ages of the victims of human trafficking mentioned in the book are altered to protect their identities.

The contents of this book are as follows: the introduction, "Human trafficking in globalized society," which attempts to look at a general view of the present situation of human trafficking overall. In the introduction, several theoretical tools are explained, so that they might help with a better understanding of the human trafficking which occurs in Cambodia. The attempt to grasp the complete picture of how and why human trafficking occurs in the country does not end in just the analysis of individual cases but rather puts an emphasis on the importance of interpreting human trafficking in Cambodia from a broader perspective. The issue of human trafficking in Cambodia has a profound connection with its social structure, which has been established on the basis of the traditional gender code, and the social norms deeply rooted in the mentality of both men and women in the country, and passed down through generations.

Following, then, is chapter 1: "Victims of Human Trafficking in the Rural Village: A Definition of the Vulnerable Family," and chapter 2: "Victims of Human Trafficking along the Cambodian–Thai Border: Who Are They?" The cases of human trafficking in Cambodia can be categorized generally into two types: the one which occurs in the rural village and the other in the border area. Chapter 1 deals with individual cases of victims of human trafficking where the victims originally belonged to rural villages. Chapter 2 takes up mainly those in the border area. The actual situation of victimized persons of human trafficking is considered from a wide range of perspectives such as historical background, geographical environment, the features and types of the members of village community, and relations with others. Methods used in human trafficking have features and variations typical to both areas: the rural village and the border area. Poipet, the area close to the national border with Thailand, is a hub of human trafficking business, so this is one of the most important researched places.

The third chapter, "The Modern History of Cambodia and the Present Situation of the Rural Village," explains the process of the growth of the market economy in a Cambodian village, the inequality between the urban areas and the rural villages, the social norms and human relationships in the rural village, and finally the concept of a village community. From a historical perspective, the consideration of what social and cultural structure has been formed in the rural village gives important clues to a deeper understanding of the real situation which faces trafficking victims.

Chapter 4 titled "The Victims of Human Trafficking: Analysis, Categorization, and General Description" attempts to create a general profile of victims and categorizes the features common to the victims, based on the interviews collected from those who were concerned. Focusing mainly on female victims this time, the chapter tries not only to explain their economic and social conditions but also to describe in what sense they are defined as needy. In many cases, these female victims are also victims of domestic violence. The chapter develops a discussion of the factors which involve them in human trafficking and a connection with the negative spiral created by the frequent violence within the family, which is common to these victims.

Chapter 5, "The Method of Aid and Support in the Border Area," attempts to evaluate the effectiveness and limits of aid and support provided by NGOs and international organizations working on the issue of human trafficking in the area close to the border with Thailand. It outlines the task that they are faced with and problems in need of resolution. During the decade after the initial survey, the number of smuggling and human trafficking incidents decreased through the International Border Check Point, the official route crossing the border between Cambodia and Thailand. However, in many cases, border crossings occur at places other than those legally designated.

Victims of human trafficking are often found among those who cross the border in this way. Through the survey of the border area, this chapter tries to examine in what way and at what point the social environment should be reorganized for improvement, and how it can be used in achieving economic independence of those who reside in the area.

Chapter 6, "How to Break Away from the Vicious Circle of Poverty," discusses the process of the liberation from poverty of the vulnerable, including the victims of human trafficking, and the possibility of setting themselves free from the restrictions of the social structure, which put them in a lower and weaker social position. In order for the vulnerable to liberate themselves from the restrictions imposed by the present social structure, recognizing the significance of self-awareness, self-respect and self-motivation holds the key. When vulnerable individuals develop a sense of self-help and take the first step forward building a community in which they enjoy an independence of their own, they can be confident in using their initiative in their own lives.

Sustainable development which optimally is supposed to be people-centered and aims for the achievement of regional independence is necessary for encouraging the vulnerable to set themselves free from the vicious circle of poverty. This is a plan to create a community where its members are protected from the negative effects of the existing social structure as it applies to an economic and social point of view, and to build a community which brings a sense of security with a partnership based on trust. In the context of today's globalized society, as aid and support now target a variety of people, the significance of this aid and support, and of development as well, is to be reconsidered.

Today, not only in Cambodia but also all over the world, human trafficking is rampant under the influence of structural violence. The purpose of the book is to provide as precise and detailed information as possible concerning the actual and present situation of the victims of human trafficking, who are in a socially marginalized position, yet are making efforts to liberate themselves from the poverty trap with the aid and support from supporting organizations.

Acknowledgments

I would like to extend my special thanks to Professor Jun Nishikawa, deceased, professor emeritus of Waseda University, Japan and the adviser for my academic life, for his direction for my overall study. Although I decided to work on the subject of human trafficking for my degree, sometimes I thought it was too challenging for me. I could not finish my doctoral dissertation without his advice and encouragement. I think he is more pleased with publishing this book than anyone. I am also truly grateful to Professor Kazuo Kuroda and other professors of Waseda University, and Professor Naomi Yuzawa of Rikkyo University, for their instructions and encouragement for my research and study.

As for my field research in Cambodia, I wish to offer my acknowledgment to Kasumi Nakagawa, a specialist on gender studies, for generously providing me with information and research materials on human trafficking. I also wish to express my thanks to Professor Machiko Kaida of Bunkyo Gakuin University and a director of the International Child Rights Center. I would like to thank the staff members of the NGOs, who have devoted themselves to working on the issue of human trafficking, for their support and cooperation with my research in Cambodia. I am sure that at this very moment they are combating human trafficking and ready to hold out a supporting hand to anyone who needs it. To Sophal Chea, who has worked with me for more than a decade, I am truly grateful for her help and cooperation.

I would like to convey my sincerest thanks to Machiko Buckley and Fuyuki Makino for their constant encouragement and advice, especially when I was feeling discouraged. I had the help of many people in completing this book, and I appreciate their support and encouragement. I would like to express my most heartfelt thanks to Kasey Beduhn and the board members of Lexington Books for giving me the excellent opportunity to publish the English version of my book. I would also like to extend my deep thanks to Kuniko Miyakami and Mark Gresham who helped me with the English translation without sparing any effort. The publication of this book would not have been realized without their help.

Lastly but not least, I owe my family gratitude more than I can express here for standing always by my side.

YUKO SHIMAZAKI

This book includes the results from studies funded by a scholarship from the Minae Masumoto Fund of the UN Women National Committee Japan in 2006 and Grants-in-Aid for Scientific Research (Grant-in-Aid for JSPS Fellows 2011 and 2013, and Grant-in-Aid for Young Scientists (B) 2014–2017) from the Japan Society for the Promotion of Science.

For the English translation, I secured funding from the English Academic Book Publication Support Subsidy of Waseda University. I would like to express my gratitude.

Introduction

Human Trafficking in Globalized Society

GLOBALIZATION AND HUMAN TRAFFICKING

According to the UN Office on Drugs and Crime (UNODC), the occurrence of human trafficking covers 124 countries including Japan, and its victimization ranges over as many as 152 nationalities.[1] Human trafficking has developed its worldwide networks, and there exist at least an estimated 510 routes/flows dealing with human trafficking, and 6 victims out of 10 are involved in transnational trafficking.[2] Trafficked persons are forced into "sexual exploitation," "forced labor," "removal of organs," and "slavery or practices similar to slavery." Human trafficking with exploitation as its purpose occurs on a global scale, and its victimization ranges over various categories of industries: manufacturing, agriculture, fishing, construction, and the sex industry. According to UNODC (2018), the victim profiles are 49 percent adult women, 21 percent adult men, 23 percent girls, and 7 percent boys.[3]

In actuality, numbers such as these, released by an international organization such as the United Nations, are just the tip of the iceberg because human trafficking is generally conducted behind the scene. Furthermore, after having been trafficked, victims are under constant surveillance and their freedom of action is limited so that it is not easy to grasp the situation. Thereby, it is quite challenging to make out the exact number of trafficked victims.

Making a comparison between men and women in the ratio of detected trafficked victims, the percentage of women is higher than that of men, and in particular that of girls shows a conspicuous increase. During the period 2004–2011, the change in victim profiles shows that the percentage of women decreased from 74 percent to 49 percent, whereas that of girls increased from 10 percent to 21 percent.[4] Thus, it can be pointed out that younger women and girls are more likely to be exposed to the risks of being victimized.

The percentage differences between men and women also vary according to the region where they are trafficked. Of all the regions concerned within the research, the highest percentage of victimized women and girls is found in Southeast Asia, which is the main research area for this study.[5]

With reference to the victimization of forced labor during the period 2010–2012, the percentage by region is as follows: in Africa and the Middle East, the percentage of men and boys make up 45 percent, while that of women and girls is 55 percent; in North and South America, men and boys account for 68 percent, while women and girls are 32 percent; in Southeast Asia and the Pacific, men and boys are 23 percent, whereas women and girls are 77 percent; and finally, in Europe and Central Asia, men and boys make up 69 percent, while women and girls are 31 percent.[6]

Human trafficking is being involved in "trading," or "buying and selling," and "reselling" of persons, and all the acts concerned with human trafficking are conducted by "traffickers," also known as "brokers." Trafficking has domestic routes, which then have further connections with multinational networks. In many cases, trafficked persons are moved from a rural village to a large city, which functions as a transit place. For the final destination, when it comes to crossing a national border, many victims are exposed to involvement in a crime network without being aware.

In discussing the subject of human trafficking, it is essential to take several viewpoints into account. First, from a broader perspective, it is important to focus on such structural aspects as economic gaps between nations and the social and cultural background of a country. These need to be considered from the viewpoint of today's international society. Second, it is crucial to pay close attention to the individual cases of trafficked victims and to study the circumstances they are in.

When the question of "Why are persons trafficked?" arises, it is important to think about the nature of human trafficking. In order to get a wider and better picture of the subject, it is important to find out that various problems, either social or personal, are deeply connected with structural aspects of the individual living situations of trafficked victims.

The Definition of Human Trafficking in the Palermo Protocol of the United Nations:

How Is Human Trafficking Defined?

In the year 2000, the United Nations provided *Protocol to Prevent, Suppress and Punish Trafficking in Persons, Especially Women and Children, supplementing the United Nations Convention against Transnational Organized*

Crime. This protocol is also known as the Palermo Protocol. According to its article 3 (a), the definition of human trafficking is given thus:

Use of Terms

"Trafficking in persons" shall mean the recruitment, transportation, transfer, harbouring or receipt of persons, by means of the threat or use of force or other forms of coercion, of abduction, of fraud, of deception, of the abuse of power or of a position of vulnerability or of the giving or receiving of payments or benefits to achieve the consent of a person having control over another person, for the purpose of exploitation. Exploitation shall include, at a minimum, the exploitation of the prostitution of others or other forms of sexual exploitation, forced labour or services, slavery or practices similar to slavery, servitude or the removal of organs.[7]

The definition above explains human trafficking in terms of its purpose, process, and means. The purpose of human trafficking lies in the exploitation of trafficked victims, such as sexual exploitation, forced labor, slavery, and the forced removal of organs. The process begins with the recruitment of target victims, followed by transportation or transfer, harboring (hiding a person), and receipt of persons (transferring and trading them). As regards the means, it employs fraud, deception, use of force (abuse, violence, cheating, and threat), and abuse of power.

Human trafficking is different from human smuggling. Human trafficking is the exploitation of trafficked persons and employs the use of force to meet its end. On the other hand, human smuggling is concerned with sending persons secretly and illegally into a country or out of a country. In short, it involves mainly illegal migration, and it does not include the "means" and the "exploitation," which make up the features of human trafficking. According to *Protocol against the Smuggling of Migration by Land, Sea and Air, Supplementing the United Nations Convention against Transnational Organized Crime*, Article 3 (a) explains thus: "Smuggling of migrants shall mean the procurement, in order to obtain, directly or indirectly, a financial or other material benefit, of the illegal entry of a person into a State Party of which the person is not a national or a permanent resident."[8]

However, there is a common feature between human smuggling and human trafficking in one regard: payment of brokerage fees and illegal entry into a country. With human trafficking, the purpose of which lies in the exploitation of trafficked victims, any form of "exploitation" distinguishes human trafficking from human smuggling.

THE PRESENT SITUATION OF HUMAN
TRAFFICKING IN CAMBODIA

In Cambodia, anyone can be a victim of human trafficking, regardless of age or gender. However, the incidences of trafficking women and girls stand out. Being trafficked, some of them are taken abroad. As the final destination, they are sent to such countries as Thailand, Malaysia, Indonesia, Taiwan, South Korea, China, and Japan to work in the sex industry, farming, construction, and manufacturing. In addition, human trafficking also occurs in the form of forced marriage and domestic work.

From the interviews taken for this research, it was found that some of the victimized women were sent to the sex industry internally in Cambodia and externally to such countries as Thailand and Malaysia. Generally speaking, not all Cambodians who are engaged in the sex industry are victims of human trafficking. In this research, victimized women and girls in the sex industry are understood to be the persons forced into prostitution. Other jobs are, for example, begging, domestic work, and working in a construction site.

As to the victimization of Cambodian men, some are sent internally somewhere in Cambodia. In other cases, victims are trafficked and sold overseas, and they are sent to such countries as Thailand, the Middle East, South Africa, Senegal, Fiji, and Mauritius.[9] The job categories they are forced into are deep-sea fishing, factories for processing fish, farming, and working in a construction site. Children are sold and bought to make them play a child's part beside a beggar, pretending to be a family or parent and a child. This is added to the forced labor in industries mentioned above.

Human trafficking still goes on in Cambodia in a way that is so cleverly conducted that it is hard to perceive it. In particular, the victimization of women and girls is recognized as one of the serious social issues. Based on such social awareness, this research attempts to illustrate the actual situation in which victimized women and girls live. It is also going to discuss the inner meaning of the phenomenon of poverty and oppression derived from the social structure of Cambodia.

International Measures and Domestic Countermeasures

There is a general consensus in international society about controlling human trafficking, and so far several international provisions have been acknowledged. The conventions applied to countermeasures against human trafficking are as follows: *Protocol to Prevent, Suppress and Punish Trafficking in Persons Especially Women and Children, supplementing the United Nations Convention against Transnational Organized Crime (the Palermo*

Protocol); Convention Concerning the Prohibition and *Immediate Action for the Elimination of the Worst Forms of Child Labour (ILO Convention No.182); Abolition of Forced Labour Convention (No.105); the International Convention on the Protection of the Rights of All Migrant Workers and Members of Their Families; Convention on the Rights of the Child; and Convention on the Elimination of All Forms of Discrimination against Women.* In accordance with the framework built on the consensus and the system of rules shared internationally, governments have endeavored to introduce legislation related to anti-human trafficking and improve domestic laws against it.

In 2004, the Greater Mekong Subregion (GMS) was formed by the six countries situated in the Mekong basin. Its member nations are Cambodia, China, Lao PDR, Myanmar, Thailand, and Vietnam. GMS organized the Coordinated Mekong Ministerial Initiative against Trafficking, also known as COMMIT. This is a multilateral cooperation network, based on the Memorandum of Understanding on Cooperation against Trafficking in Persons in the GMS, signed by the ministers of GMS in 2004. Along with the expansion of transnational human trafficking, the memorandum was signed by two countries and regions voluntarily among the member nations of COMMIT, for the purpose of constructing a network of cross-border cooperation and intensifying countermeasures against human trafficking.

The memorandum signed by the member nations of COMMIT has brought about a positive influence in several respects. For instance, this helped each member country to lay the foundation of improving laws relevant to human trafficking and taking more precise measures against it. As one thing that is worthy of note, COMMIT set up the project called UN Inter-Agency Project on Human Trafficking in Greater Mekong Subregion (UNIAP), in cooperation with the United Nations.[10] The international organizations joining in the project worked in close cooperation with each other. Thus, the operation of this project enabled the international organizations concerned to work on such measures as prevention, rescue, protection, improving legislation, policy responses, prosecution, monitoring, and evaluation. As a result of this, controlling measures against human trafficking made progress.

Internationally, the Cambodian government worked in cooperation with its neighboring countries. In 2003, Cambodia signed a statement of mutual agreement with the Thai government, and in 2005 with the Vietnamese government.

Internally, in the year 2000, the government of Cambodia approved *Declaration on Measures to Be Taken for the Implementation of the National Five Year Plan against Child Trafficking and Sexual Exploitation 2000–2004,*

xxiv   *Introduction*

Royal Government of Cambodia,[11] and also took measures for prevention, protection, and prosecution against human trafficking.

In 2003, a taskforce was organized to take action on human trafficking under the leadership of the Ministry of Women, working together with the Ministries of Justice, Education, Youth and Sports, Social Affairs, Veterans and Youth Rehabilitation, Interior (state police), and Health.[12] In addition, the Ministry of Tourism set up the project of the Child Safe Tourism Commission, in cooperation with World Vision Cambodia, international NGOs, together with local NGOs, with the aim of preventing foreign tourists not only from having sex with children but also from sightseeing with sexual purposes. The project also developed a publicity campaign and did leafleting. Since then, the ministries concerned, international organizations, and NGOs have been working together in close cooperation to promote countermeasures against human trafficking.

The Law Relevant to Human Trafficking in Cambodia

Looking at the laws related to punishment for human trafficking in Cambodia, the Constitution of the Kingdom of Cambodia stipulates in Article 31 of chapter 3 thus: "The Kingdom of Cambodia recognizes and respects . . . women's rights and children's rights"[13] and Article 45 says that "all forms of discrimination against women shall be abolished. . . . Men and women are equal in all fields especially with respect to marriage and family matters."[14] Article 46 speaks that "trading human beings, the exploitation of prostitution and obscenity, which affect the reputation of women, shall be prohibited."[15]

Another example of the relevant laws is *Provisions Relating to the Judiciary and Criminal Law* and *Procedure applicable in Cambodia during the Transitional Period*, also known as the UNTAC Criminal Law. This is the law promulgated and enforced by the Supreme National Council in 1992. During its provisional government, UNTAC made a proposal for establishing the Supreme National Council, and it was prescribed in one of the provisions approved by the Paris Peace Agreement. The members of the council were the representatives of the political parties engaged in the Cambodian Civil War.

UNTAC Criminal Law, Article 41, speaks about "assault and battery."[16]Article 42 stipulates "indecent assault"[17] and its clause 3 says that "any person who procures, entices or leads away, for purposes of prostitution, or exploits the prostitution of a minor, even with the consent of that minor, shall be liable to a term of imprisonment for two to six years."[18] Article 35 refers to "illegal confinement"[19] saying, "Anyone who, without orders from the judicial authority, arrests, detains or illegally confines anyone shall be liable to imprisonment."[20]

Nonetheless, it can be said that the series of laws were probably inadequate to punish and control human trafficking. Thus, in order to supplement the series of laws, the *Law on Suppression of the Kidnapping, Trafficking and Exploitation of Human Persons* was adopted on the 16th of January in 1996. It was promulgated and took effect on the 26th of February in the same year.

This law consists of five chapters with ten articles altogether: chapter 1 is General Provision; chapter 2, Kidnapping of Human Persons for Trafficking; chapter 3, Pimping; chapter 4, Debauchery; and chapter 5, Final Provision. Article 3 clause 1 says that anyone who commits human trafficking "even though upon there is or no consent from the concerned person, by ways of forcing, threatening or using of hypnotic drugs, in order to kidnap him/her for trafficking sale or for prostitution, shall be subject to imprisonment from ten (10) to fifteen (15) years."[21] It also says that anyone who traffics minors "shall be punished by imprisonment from fifteen (15) to twenty (20) years, in the case that the victim is a minor person of less than 15 years old."[22]

Before the law of suppression of human trafficking, enacted in 1996, the government of Cambodia had already ratified the following: *Convention of Child's Rights*; *Convention on the Elimination of All Forms of Discrimination against Women*; and *Protocol to Prevent, Suppress and Punish Trafficking in Persons, Especially Women and Children, Supplementing the United Nations Convention against Transnational Organized Crime*.

However, in actuality, the law enforced in 1996 did not follow adequately the substance of these conventions, if considered from the viewpoint of international standards. To deal with the evermore complicated situation of human trafficking, it was necessary for the Cambodian government to meet international standards. Thus, the government established a more comprehensive law in 2008: *The Law on Suppression of Human Trafficking and Sexual Exploitation*.[23]

Nevertheless, in Cambodia, there still exist various obstacles to enforce the laws relevant to controlling human trafficking.[24] This is also partly because bribes are offered to offenders, judges, and prosecutors. Such dishonesty is likely to undermine the fairness in investigation, indictment, proceedings, and judgment.[25]

In order to strengthen the control of human trafficking, needless to say, it is essential to enact more comprehensive laws so as to conform to the actual situation. It is also necessary to develop a social campaign to make people intensely aware of the risks of human trafficking, the social environment causing human trafficking, and the process of its victimization. The majority of trafficked victims live in severe living conditions. Thus, it is desirable to include remedial action for economic poverty and relative poverty in human trafficking controlling measures. From a global perspective, it should be emphasized that Cambodia needs to tighten cooperation with the international society.

Theoretical Tools to Interpret the Situation of Human Trafficking in Cambodia

Theoretical tools provide a framework for looking at human trafficking from its structural aspect. From a broader perspective, knowledge of international relations can be helpful. In addition, understanding the social and cultural background of Cambodia is essential, as it is a thorough consideration from the viewpoint of today's international society.

Leading researchers of earlier studies are G. Lerner, K. Barry, and T. D. Truong. First, Lerner analyzed a relationship between slavery and violence against women. Second, Barry made an analysis of human trafficking of women in the sex industry. Finally, Truong studied the relationship between labor migration and the sex industry. There are also other positive studies concerning how human trafficking occurs and expands in a large scale of labor migration. However, based on the interviews and observation conducted by the present author, understanding the victimizing process of human trafficking in Cambodia probably needs to consider such factors as the structural violence inherent in Cambodian society, the gender code, and the structure of centralization and marginalization in Cambodia.

Through the expansion of globalization, the market economy has extended to rural parts of Southeast Asia. As a result, the spread of the market economy generates poverty, gender inequality, and a social environment in which socially vulnerable people are involved in human trafficking. It should be emphasized that the subject of human trafficking needs to be considered from this socially and culturally dynamic point of view.

Analysis of the situation of human trafficking in Cambodia employs several basic theories: world system theory, gender, and the concept of structural violence by Johan Galtung. Finally, the theory of capability by Amartya Sen provides a theoretical framework for defining poverty in terms of the deprivation of human rights. The knowledge of these basic theories provides a broader perspective in interpreting the situation of human trafficking. They also aid in the understanding of how human trafficking occurs, how and why socially vulnerable people are influenced by negative factors derived from social structure, and in what way their human rights are violated or deprived. At the same time, the issue of human trafficking can be considered from these viewpoints. It leads to discovering the reason why women and girls are turned into trafficked victims and the connection between poverty and social structure. It allows the consideration of the vulnerability of trafficked victims and their family situation.

THE CONCEPT OF STRUCTURAL VIOLENCE:
VIOLENCE GENERATED FROM SOCIAL STRUCTURE

J. Galtung[26] produces the concept of structural violence as a theoretical tool in order to analyze a world in which poverty and oppression exist, not in the form of a quantitative theory, but in the form of analysis of the structural cause of violence. It is the concept of structural violence that is the key to this theory. It explains that when people are afflicted by discrimination and social oppression, it is because of violence attributed to the social structure.

Galtung defines violence in two ways: violence in a narrow sense and that in a broader sense. The former is called "direct violence," and is a brutal act with the intention of hurting or damaging someone physically or mentally. Its performer is visible and identifiable. The latter is different from "direct violence" in the sense that its performer is invisible and cannot be specified, and physical force is not used with the intention of damaging someone.[27] *Structural violence* is the term used to interpret the situation in which the social structure itself inflicts negative effects such as discrimination and social oppression.

For instance, structural violence arises from social structure in the form of inequality of opportunities in life. It is also recognized as unfairness in a power relationship. Fundamentally, everyone is entitled to the right to life, social rights, and cultural rights, and everyone has the capability of self-realization within themselves. Each person should be allowed not only to have these basic rights but also to achieve self-realization in their own way. However, when they are deprived of their rights or they are denied opportunities by social and cultural reasons, the scope of individual capabilities becomes smaller. This can be understood as structural violence.

Structural violence is recognizable as the unfair treatment of educational and medical services between different social groups or areas. When social relations intensify social inequality and imbalance, discrimination and prejudice, and poverty, it is likely that violations of human rights will ensue. Once these social relations become established, structural violence remains constant because it is already inherent in the social structure which creates these social relations.

The figure 0.1 shows the relationship between human trafficking and structural violence. First, trafficked victims and their families come from a social environment in which they are deprived of their basic rights and opportunities in life because of the social structure. Second, within the society built on the basis of human relationship in the neighborhood, they are excluded from a mutual support system or a community network existing in a regional community, and then they are isolated from the other members, either individually or in a group. Poverty is partly caused by the situation in which they suffer from social exclusion and the deprivation of their rights and opportunities.

Under the circumstances, poverty is maintained or is intensified by structural violence. As the result of this, it is highly probable that these isolated and needy people are made victims of human trafficking.

A DEFINITION OF POVERTY

As stated by A. Sen, poverty is not necessarily determined by the shortage of income as "income poverty" but something that is explained based on the concept of deprivation. Basically, everyone is entitled to the right to food, clothing, and housing; the right to have an education; and the right to have medical care and good health. According to Sen, *Entitlement* is the term used to explain the state in which all people everywhere should have rights and opportunities in life, and people freely build relations with others.[28] *Functionings* refers to the state in which people lead their lives by enjoying these rights, utilizing their opportunities and doing various activities.[29]

However, people are put in a socially vulnerable position when they are denied freedom of action and when they are deprived of their basic rights and opportunities of self-realization. For example, if someone's entitlement lacks sufficient food and necessary nutrition, the person will suffer from hunger.[30] In addition, when an individual or a group of people suppress others' rights and opportunities in life, the entitlement of the oppressed people is undermined. In this case, it can be the cause of poverty or hunger.[31]

People have combinations of various basic activities in leading their lives, and the quality of life is enhanced when they achieve them. This is explained

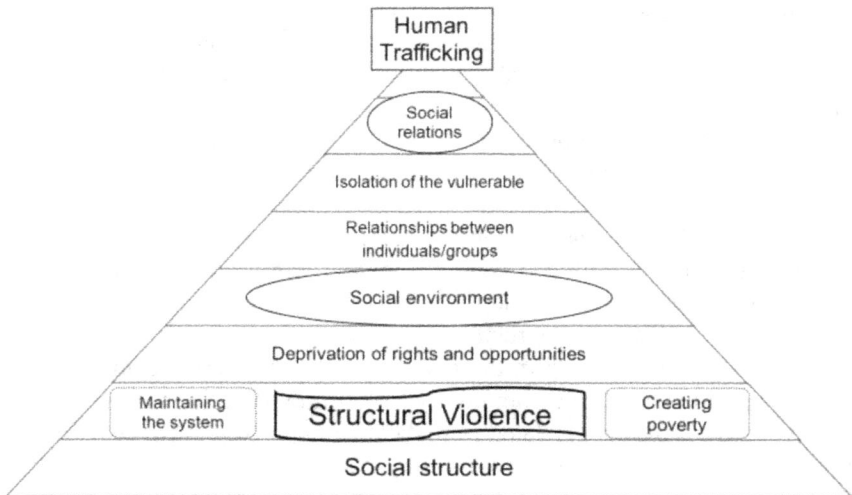

Figure 0.1   Relationships between Human Trafficking and Structural Violence.

as *functionings* by Sen.[32] As one thing that is worthy of note, fundamentally the theory of capabilities focuses on basic needs, individual rights, and opportunities in life. It also adopts an original approach in dealing with the range of functionings achievable by individuals' voluntary actions.[33] The theory includes the environment and situation in which people live, and additionally, social relations people build in its theoretical framework. According to the theory, the scope for opportunities in life can be gradually expanded by achieving self-realization. Then it encourages individuals to improve their quality of life. In other words, "well-being" is achievable by extending the range of their functionings, as stated by Sen.[34]

In looking at the relationship between poverty and trafficked victims, these broader perspectives probably help to grasp the whole situation of human trafficking. For instance, as is often the case, trafficked victims are sent back to the places of their origin after being taken into protection. However, this cannot always be the final solution for them, since the problem of how they can emerge from their poverty still remains. For those who are in a marginalized position within the existing social structure, temporal supports are not necessarily sufficient for improving their living environment. This is partly because the environment in which they had lived before being trafficked is still in need of improvement in an economic and social sense. Thus, even though they go back to their original places, it is probable that they will face the same situation as before, where they suffer from poverty and other problems related to it. In considering how they can break away from poverty, it is important to work on improving their living conditions from general aspects. First, these vulnerable people should have their basic rights restored to enjoy, and their social environment accordingly should be improved in terms of defending their human rights. Second, enhanced conditions are to be sustained. Finally, it is necessary for individuals to take action for their self-actualization, making use of advantages and opportunities offered by the improved environment.

The Social Phenomenon: The Majority of the Poor Are Women and Girls: Social Structure and "Feminization of Poverty"

The majority of the economically underprivileged are women and girls in a society in which they are in a position with less power and authority in the context of power relationships. This is a phenomenon explained as the "feminization of poverty." Attention to the concept of "feminization of poverty" was drawn at the United Nations World Conference on Women in the 1980s.[35] The circumstances of women in developing countries can be considered by connecting the feminization of poverty with World System Theory. Women's poverty and class distinction is the product of the social system in which they live. Moreover, it is also the result of relations between developing and developed nations, a global imbalance of capitalism, the influence of social structure, and achievements of social and economic development in developing nations.

In actuality, poverty cannot be reduced only by achieving economic growth. As far as the present situation of developing countries is concerned, the more economic policies are implemented, the wider the disparity between rich and poor. As a result, the poor and needy are put in a severer economic situation.

It is necessary to acknowledge that poverty existing in modern society results not only from the present economic situation but also from social stratification, and it has been embraced within the social structure. The factors developing social stratification are, for example, economic divide, social discrimination, cultural prejudice, and political dominance and subordination. These social factors include race, region, gender, and generation, and they reciprocally influence each other. Eventually people's social relations and power relationship are determined by the interaction between them. According to the degree of power and authority, a social hierarchy is formed, and a socially vulnerable group is settled at its bottom.

Poverty is not something that is generated spontaneously but rather artificially produced and accumulated through the workings of social relations. What breeds poverty are economic status, discrimination and prejudice against being poor, social isolation, and the relationship between domination and subordination. The deprivation of human rights is correlatively related to discrimination and inequality between social classes.

In particular, in a male-oriented authoritarian society, or a patriarchy, women and girls are subordinate to men and are settled in a lower social position from the viewpoint of gender. In many cases, socially discriminated women and girls are denied their human rights and suffer from poverty. This is a phenomenon which is described as the feminization of poverty. The fact that the majority of victims of human trafficking are women and girls represents a part of the feminization of poverty. In the United Nations, human trafficking in women and girls is regarded as a form of "violence against women." The feminization of poverty can be recognized in various parts of Cambodian society. From the viewpoint of poverty of women, human trafficking in Cambodian women and girls is going to be considered through the examination of individual cases.

NOTES

1. The UN Office on Drugs and Crime (UNODC), *Global Report on Trafficking in Persons 2014* (New York, NY: United Nations, 2014), 5, 7, 17. The data cited in the text refers to the occurrence of human trafficking during the period 2010–2012.

According to this report, the total number of victims analyzed by UNDOC is 40,177 persons. The number of suspects of human trafficking is 33,860. Of these, 34,256 were prosecuted, and 13,310 were punished.

2. Ibid., 5, 8, 37.

3. UNODC, *Global Report on Trafficking in Persons 2018* (New York, NY: United Nations, 2018), 10. The report released by the International Labour Organization (ILO), in 2017; the total number of people held in modern slavery in 2016 was an estimated 40.3 million. The breakdown of victims estimated that 24.9 million or more victims were involved in forced labor and 15.4 million in forced marriage. Moreover women and girls are disproportionately affected by modern slavery, accounting for 28.7 million, or 71 percent of the overall total (ILO, *Global Estimates of Modern Slavery* [Geneva: ILO, 2017], 10). The ILO categorizes two types of modern slavery: forced labor and forced marriage, with forced labor divided into (1) state-imposed forced labur, (2) forced labor exploitation, and (3) forced sexual exploitation of adults and commercial sexual exploitation of children (ILO, *Global Estimates of Modern Slavery*, 16–17).

4. UNODC, *Global Report on Trafficking in Persons 2014*, 31.

5. Ibid., 36.

6. Ibid.

7. *Protocol to Prevent, Suppress and Punish Trafficking in Persons, Especially Women and Children, Supplementing the United Nations Convention against Transnational Organized Crime* (New York, NY: The United Nations, 2000).

8. *Protocol against the Smuggling of Migration by Land, Sea and Air, Supplementing the United Nations Convention against Transitional Organized Crime.*

9. Counter Trafficking in Persons Project (CTIP II), *Where Is the Horizon?* (Phnom Penh: CTIP II, 2014), 2. The research conducted by the author also reached the same results as the data from CTIP regarding the regions where the victims are trafficked and sold overseas.

10. The project by UNIAP was divided into three periods: first, from 2002 to 2003; second, from 2003 to 2006; and finally from 2006 to 2009. Its activities were engaged in projects on a small scale in connection with each other, organizing working plans of each participating nation and administrating the scheme. After the project by UNIAP was completed, The UN Actions for Cooperation against Trafficking Persons (UN-ACT) took over the series of assignments and activities based on the network built by UNIAP. UN-ACT is a regional project managed by the United Nations Development Programme (UNDP). UN-ACT works with a range of networks and partners by UN agencies and NGOs. UN-ACT is building the capacity of regional and national actors, including governments, civil society, and frontline responders, to work in a more effective and concerted manner (http://un-act.org/what/. Accessed January 20, 2020). See http://un-act.org/.

11. *Declaration on Measures to Be Taken for the Implementation of the National Five Year Plan against Child Trafficking and Sexual Exploitation 2000–2004* (Royal Government of Cambodia, No. 01S.Pr. K).

12. With regard to the series of actions in the taskforce chronologically, in 2002, the Department of Anti-Human Trafficking and Juvenile Protection was set up in

the Ministry of Interior, which was followed by the taskforce in 2003. In 2005, the Ministry of Women's Affairs took the lead in intensifying and consolidating the network of Coordinated Mekong Ministerial Initiative against Trafficking (COMMIT). In 2011, Department of Anti-Human Trafficking and Reintegration was set up within Ministry of Social Affairs, Veterans and Youth Rehabilitation (MoSVY).

13. *The Constitution of Kingdom of Cambodia*, 1993, https://cambodia.ohchr.or g/~cambodiaohchr/sites/default/files/Constitution_ENG.pdf (accessed January 27, 2020).

14. Ibid.

15. Ibid.

16. *Provisions Relating to the Judiciary and Criminal Law and Procedure Applicable in Cambodia during the Transitional Period, 1992* (Accessed January 27, 2020), https://www.wto.org/english/thewto_e/acc_e/khm_e/WTACCKHM3A3 _LEG_11.pdf

17. Ibid.

18. Ibid.

19. Ibid.

20. Ibid.

21. *Law on Suppression of the Kidnapping, Trafficking and Exploitation of Human Persons (1996)* (Accessed January 27, 2020), https://www.ilo.org/dyn/natlex/docs/ ELECTRONIC/59890/60877/F65566

22. Ibid.

23. *NS/RKM/0208/005 on the Suppression of Human Trafficking and Sexual Exploitation. Adopted on: 2007-12-20*, https://www.unodc.org/res/cld/document/k hm/2008/law_on_suppression_of_human_trafficking_and_sexual_exploitation_htm l/Cambodia_03_-_Law-on-Suppression-of-Human-Trafficking-and-Sexual-Exploita tion-15022008-Eng.pdf (accessed January 27, 2020).

24. For example, the Chai Hour II Hotel Incident in Phnom Penh in December 2004. This was criticized then by the international society. Cambodia Human Rights Action Committee (CHRAC) had a press release and issued a statement about the issues. http://www.licadho-cambodia.org/press/files/80statementCHHotel.pdf, and European parliament resolution on trafficking of women and children in Cambodia (B6-0045/2005), (accessed June 5, 2020).

25. Kenji Yotsumoto, In Other Words, 2004, 191. An interview conducted by the author also found the same opinions concerning the matter.

26. Johan Galtung, In Other Words, 1991.

27. Ibid., 5.

28. Entitlements defined by Sen as "the set of alternative commodity bundles that a person can command in a society using the totality of rights and opportunities that he or she faces" (Amartya Sen, *Resources, Values and Development* [Cambridge, MA and London: Harvard University Press, 1984], 497). "the focus on entitlement has the effect of emphasizing legal rights" (Amartya Sen, *Poverty and Famine* [Oxford: University Press, 1981, Reprinted 2013], [1984], [1992], 165–66). "The law stands between food availability and food entitlement. Starvation deaths can reflect legality with a vengeance" (Sen, *Poverty and Famine*, 166), and Sen explained that

"Entitlement refers to set of alternative commodity bundles that a person can command in a society using the totality of rights and opportunities that he or she faces" (Sen, *Resources, Values and Development*, 497).

29. "The various combinations of functionings (being and doing) that the person can achieve" (Amartya Sen, *Inequality Reexamined* [New York, NY: Oxford University Press, 1992, Reprinted 2009], 40).

30. see Sen, *Resources, Values and Development*; and Jun Nishikawa, *Ningen no tame no keizaigaku* (Economics for People) (Tokyo: Iwanami Shoten, 2000), 303.

31. Nishikawa, 303.

32. Sen, *Inequality Reexamined*. "The functionings included can vary from the most elementary ones, such as being well-nourished, avoiding escapable morbidity and premature mortality, and so on, to quite complex and sophisticated achievements, such as having self-respect, being able to take part in the life of the community, and so on" (Sen, *Inequality Reexamined*, 5).

33. Sen, *Inequality Reexamined*; Sen, *Resources, Values and Development*.

34. Sen, *Poverty and Famine*.

35. Started with the third world conference on women in Nairobi, with the key words of "equality," "development," and "peace" for achieving "sustainable development," the following conferences were held in succession: World Conference on Women in 1991 (Global Assembly of Women and the Environment, and world Women's Congress for a Healthy Planet, both held in Miami); World Conference on Human Rights in Vienna, 1993; Conference on International Conference on Population and Development in Cairo, 1994; and World Summit for Social Development in Copenhagen, 1995. In the series of conferences, the platform and strategies for the advocacy of women's human rights were declared. At the same time, the structural aspect of "violence against women" drew public attention, and it led to the adoption of "The Elimination of Violence against Women" in the UN General assembly in 1993.

Chapter 1

Victims of Human Trafficking in the Rural Village

A Definition of the Vulnerable Family

The primary aim of this chapter is to attempt to grasp how vulnerable individuals and families become caught up in human trafficking, giving consideration to how it occurs, and to better understand the actual situation of the families of trafficked victims. By taking up actual incidents of human trafficking which occurred in the rural villages in Cambodia, the cases of the victims' families are examined by closely focusing on the individual family situations, and reviewing the connection between social structure and the circle of poverty.

THE BACKGROUND OF THE SEPARATION OF FAMILY BROUGHT ABOUT BY MIGRATION AND THE CAUSE OF BEING TRAPPED IN HUMAN TRAFFICKING

In Cambodia, migration has now become part of general practice commonly conducted in various areas around the country either for a long term or a short one. The case of a sixteen year old girl called Sophia provides an example of how the separation from family resulted in her being trafficked. Furthermore, her case explains that she was also a victim of the circle of poverty which ended up putting her entire family into a more socially and economically vulnerable position than ever before. This chapter attempts to consider first, what connection can be found between the separation from family caused by migration and an individual becoming a trafficked victim from a marginalized situation; second, what caused a vulnerable family like hers to fall into the poverty trap after a series of migration and human trafficking incidents.

1

View of a Village. *Source*: ©Yuko Shimazaki.

Case Study: Sophia (sixteen years old)

(Her name has been changed to protect her identity, as will be the case for
all interviewees.)

The Family Situation

Her father once found a job in fishing in Thailand as a migrant worker. While
working in Thailand, he fell ill and returned to the village of his origin. Later,
he became bedridden and eventually died. The money he had earned from his
migrant labor was allotted to his medical treatment, but this was not enough
to cover the entire cost. Thus, the family had to continually borrow money.
The amount owed gradually increased, and the mother had to find a job in
Thailand to pay off the debt, while she arranged for her daughters, Sophia and
her elder sister, to be taken care of at her relatives' place.

The Situation of Sophia and Her Sister after
Being Taken to the Relatives

As soon as the mother left for Thailand, Sophia and her sister came to the
place of their mother's relatives whom they had never met before. The relatives had plenty of food and daily commodities, and they had enough money
to lend to others. Their aunt dressed gorgeously and wore expensive jewelry.

The living conditions the sisters saw at their relatives' were completely opposite to their own. Part of money their mother sent from Thailand would be for the sisters' education and living expenses. However, the sisters were not given enough food and were put in a harsh environment.

The mother probably took ill while working in Thailand, and every time she returned home she was worse than the previous time. In their village, the neighbors talked about their mother, saying that she must have been HIV-positive. As a result, Sophia and her sister became the target of discriminatory remarks and were ignored by the people in the village. They did not know whether their mother was truly HIV-positive or not; yet they devoted themselves to nursing her. In spite of the daughters' dedicated nursing, their mother died in 2003.

The wishes of the deceased mother were for her relatives to allot the money she earned in Thailand for her daughters' education. Nevertheless, the promise was not kept. After their mother's death, Sophia and her sister appealed to their relatives to go to school, but they would not let them do so. Instead, the sisters were forced to do housekeeping at their relatives' place. There they were often the victims of acts of violence from their relatives, both physically and mentally.

The Situation of Sophia's Sister and Violence against Her

Soon after the sisters' mother died, a friend of their relatives paid frequent visits to them, and proposed they should find a job in Thailand and work there, saying he could get them a job selling fruit. Their uncle often suggested that Sophia's sister should go to Thailand for the job, and in the end she was persuaded to go as a migrant worker.

Sophia was told by her sister that in reality she would not like to go to Thailand, but there was no other choice but to do so. Their uncle and the friend of his made all the preparation for sending the sister to Thailand. Later, Sophia learned that their uncle took her sister to Thailand and saw her off there.

Her sister came back home from Thailand only once, but she never told what she did and where she stayed. Sophia said that her sister never answered her questions about what had happened to her, and instead begged her younger sister not to ask about her any more. Sophia felt it so strange, but every time she tried to ask for information about her elder sister, she felt sad and embarrassed, so she decided not to inquire any longer.

Sophia never heard from her sister after this one time she returned home and went back to Thailand. The village people came to know this, and they started to talk about her sister saying that she must have been trafficked to a brothel and infected with HIV. Sophia asked her aunt and uncle about what had happened to her sister, but they only said that they knew nothing about her. Thinking they must have kept something about her sister secret, Sophia started to become suspicious of them. She had no idea if her sister was still alive or not, and had never spent even a single day without missing her.

After her sister was sent to Thailand, Sophia was left alone with her relatives who escalated their acts of physical and mental violence against her, keeping her always afraid of the behavior of her aunt and uncle. One day she went out for help from others in the village, but they would not try to help in front of her aunt and uncle because they were afraid of her relatives' power. According to Sophia, her aunt and uncle were said to have been involved in illegal activities before, and that was probably the reason why the village members were reluctant to offer her some help. On a daily basis Sophia was beaten with a wooden stick or a belt, and sometimes kicked and hit on the back with an iron stick. The bruises and scars on her body proved well enough that she was a frequent victim of violence.

Now that she had never heard from her sister, Sophia was ordered to go and work there by her aunt and uncle. When her uncle's friend visited her, Sophia was told that the work she was supposed to do was a housekeeping job and that she would know the location of the work once she got to the country. On hearing that, she became fearful that she might be trafficked just like her sister. While continuing their physical violence against Sophia, her relatives made preparation for her to go to Thailand against her will. Some neighbors, thinking that there was something wrong and feeling suspicious of human trafficking, reported this incident to an NGO that immediately took protective action for her.

The Separation of Family Brought about by the Migration of the Head of a Family and the Negative Spiral of Poverty

From this case of Sophia it can be said that migration does not necessarily turn the economic and social situation of a poor family for the better. Despite the fact that the father migrated with the hope of bringing a better life to his family, the family only got the unfortunate consequence of the cost of his medical treatment and the ballooning debt to cover it, and finally, the loss of the main breadwinner and the shift to a fatherless family. All of these factors contributed to worsening the poverty they were faced with.

Following the father's death, other family members had to set out for migration in order to gain cash for paying back the debt the father left. Without owning any property, Sophia and the others had no other job alternatives except for working by the day. As a result of this, the mother decided to find a job in Thailand. Sophia and her sister, with no adult person to take care of them in their family, were left with relatives of their mother. This series of consequences the family went through ended up making their economic conditions worse than before.

Sophia in actuality had no idea what kind of job her mother was engaged in. Similar to the situation with her father, her mother was probably taken ill while working in Thailand, and every time she came back home, she got worse than before, just like her father did. When the neighbors came to know of this, they started to treat her coldly—a target of discrimination and prejudice with unkind remarks about her mother's migration. Contrary to this, when her father became ill, the neighbors expressed their sympathy toward him.

This reaction is not unique to Sophia's family but also to other examples of female migration in general. There still is a tendency to label female migrant workers as losers when they fail to earn enough money to meet the expectations of their families, and when they return home with illness, the situation can be so much the worse for them. From this, it can be inferred that in Cambodia the degree of expectations from the family is much higher for female migrant workers than for males—female workers are counted on more as the ones who will bring economic improvement to the family.

When a female worker has done anything against the gender code embraced in the rural society of Cambodia, the community members are likely to take a hostile attitude toward her. As in the case of Sophia's mother when she became ill, the villagers labeled her as having been a prostitute in Thailand and HIV-positive, and their suspicious and unfriendly attitude extended to Sophia and her sister because in the rural village at that time there was still no precise knowledge of HIV.

These prejudices are particularly common in villages in Cambodia, and if a female worker falls ill, the neighbors are likely to take her as a sex worker and make discriminatory remarks about her, especially for poor people. This is one of the reasons why female workers are unwilling to go back to the villages of their origin. As they are completely mentally and physically fatigued from working in a foreign country or away from home, there is little energy left in them to confront and cope with such harsh situations. Also they are afraid of being regarded as a failure, so they are strongly conscious of the sense that they have to make as much money as possible. In the interviews taken in the village, not a few women said that they had to be successful bringing much cash to their family, lest they become the target of unkind remarks in the neighborhood if they failed to produce enough money.

It is necessary to bear in mind that migration by a spouse or a family member does not always end up in successfully turning the family situation for the better. On the contrary, in some cases it is likely to aggravate the problem of poverty resulting in the consequences of turning the economic and social situation of the family for the worse.

Social Environment of Orphans

The death of their parents helped to worsen the situation in which Sophia and her sister lived. Their relatives had taken the money their deceased mother left to them and had never given them enough food. Despite the fact that the sisters asked them to let them have a formal education, they would not allow it. Physically and mentally they were victims of acts of violence on a daily basis and were put in the situation of human deprivation. They were beaten with a wooden stick or a belt, kicked and hit on the back with an iron stick. For their relatives, the sisters were simply a gold mine, and such inhumane treatment violated the fundamental human rights of the sisters.

As mentioned earlier, after the separation from her sister, Sophia was left alone and was made the sole target of violence and of other callous acts such as depriving her of the basic rights to food, clothing, and housing. Trapped into a vicious spiral, Sophia was now taken captive and enslaved against her will.

Migration by any one member of a family is a common practice in Cambodia, and many cases of human trafficking, together with the separation from family and problems with human rights violations, occur all around Cambodia. Still, Sophia's case may be categorized as a particularly bad one because multiple incidents happened to her alone in sequence: the death of

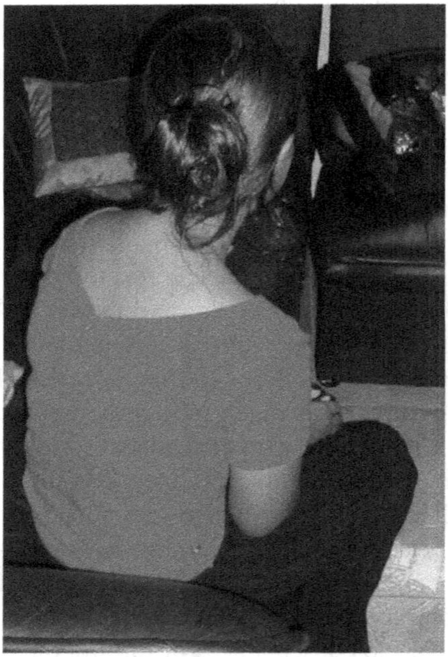

Victim of Human Trafficking. *Source*: ©Yuko Shimazaki.

her parents; the separation of her only sibling; violence, enslavement, discrimination, and prejudice against migrant labor; and prejudice toward her mother and sister labeled as prostitutes and HIV-positives.

Each incident Sophia went through, without doubt, deserves to be examined in analyzing the factors which led to her being trafficked. Moreover, studying the process in which she had to bear the harsh circumstances of the violation of her human rights and dignity can be worthy of consideration. Taking up the sequence of events Sophia experienced will help in understanding how a vulnerable person could fall into the very depth of the vicious spiral of poverty against his or her will because of structural violence inherent in society. At the bottom of the social hierarchy, the reproduction of poverty is generated by a negative chain reaction in which the result of the previous incident becomes the cause of the following one.

RELATIONSHIP BETWEEN POVERTY AND SEXUAL VIOLENCE

Isolation in the village increases the risk of becoming a victim of human trafficking. Presented here is the case of a woman who was made a discriminatory target after sexual violence in her home village, was abandoned by her family, and had to leave the village of her origin. To be more precise, this section attempts to explain how a woman called Kuntiah (her name has been changed to protect her identity) having been raped in the village exercised influence on her and her family, and led to human trafficking.

Case Study: Kuntiah (twenty years old)

Family Members and Family Situation

Her family consisted of her parents and three sisters, and Kuntiah was the youngest. The parents and the eldest sister had chronic illnesses, so their physical condition would not allow them to work. The second sister was a migrant worker, engaged in a housekeeping job in Thailand, but they had never received money from her. Since her childhood, on a daily basis Kuntiah was a victim of domestic violence, having been kicked and beaten with a wooden stick. After she was raped in her home village, her parents became more violent toward her than ever before.

Work and Debt

Kuntiah's family made their living by receiving some vegetables for free from their neighbors and selling them in the market. When they could not get vegetables, they earned their living as day laborers in the market and by fishing or begging, and they earned as much as 3000 riel (75 US cents then).[1] They borrowed 500,000 riel (US$125 then) for the father's medical treatment. Their debt amounted to 700,000 riel (US$175 then) including interest added to the initial debt of 500,000 riel. They actually had no prospect for paying it off. They just counted on the money which probably the second sister would send from Thailand, but it was disappointing. Consequently their debt was mounting.

Receiving Sexual Violence

When she was seventeen years old, Kuntiah was raped by a man who came to the village as a migrant worker. He intimidated her from ever talking about the incident. At the age of eighteen, she was attacked from behind and raped again. She was told by the attacker that she was so poor that she could do nothing about it and would have to put up with the situation, and if she reported to the police, they would not believe her because she was poor.

Eventually, she could not bear the pain of having been raped twice and told her parents about it. On listening to her, her parents became ashamed. Although they reported to the police about what happened to their daughter, there was no sign of improvement in the situation. Soon after, the story that she was a victim of sexual violence went around the village. The family had already been made a target of discriminatory remarks about their poverty by the neighboring people even before she was raped, but once they came to know of the rape, they kept away from the family. So there were no friends for the family to count on in the village.

Human Trafficking

When Kuntiah was selling vegetables in the market as usual, a man whom she knew approached her asking her if she should like to go to Poipet, telling her that she could earn as much money as 2,500 baht (US$60 then)[2] a day. As she was isolated from her family after the rape incident and was a frequent victim of domestic violence, she wished to go out of the village if she could. So Kuntiah thought that there would not be a better chance than this, and decided to take it.

However, in actuality, the place she was taken by the man who offered her the job was not Poipet but a brothel in Thailand. The route they followed to get to the brothel was from her home village to Poipet, the area close to the border between Cambodia and Thailand, and then from Poipet to a transit place in Thailand. After entry into Thailand, she was finally taken to the brothel, with the final destination kept secret from her. At the brothel, when she refused to engage in prostitution, the owner, or the employer, used violence to intimidate her and put drugs in every meal she ate. At the beginning, she never thought about why she felt somewhat drowsy and sluggish, but eventually she realized that she had been drugged. She was kept in a locked room and was never paid.

The Financial Situation of a Victim of Human Trafficking and Sexual Violence

Kuntiah's family was a needy one with daily income somewhere between 2000 riel and 3000 riel, less than US$1 and under the poverty line. They suffered a constant shortage of food, as they owned no land property and could not be self-sufficient in food. Kuntiah was raped twice: the first time was when she was seventeen, and the second time when she was eighteen years of age. In both cases the situation in which she was raped was very similar: after she was attacked from behind and raped, she was forbidden to talk about it under threat of violence. According to her, the man who attacked her would have thought that she was too poor to be able to do anything helpful for herself and that she would not go to the police. From the viewpoint of the social structure, the voices of socially vulnerable people like her would be silenced and not heard again. This is structural violence, and it often removes these have-nots from society into obscurity.

When Kuntiah's family reported the rape to the police, their neighbors came to know about it and started to exhibit an unfriendly attitude toward them. However, contrary to Kuntiah's case, in some interviews with rape victims there were some positive cases where they were helped out by neighbors, and the perpetrator was found. In one case the village leader took immediate measures, which led to the arrest of the criminal. There was also a case in which villagers found the criminal and put him on trial. In cases such as these, the incident of sexual violence does not lead to human trafficking.[3]

On one hand, there is a case where the criminal was arrested and was put on trial through the united efforts of the villagers. On the other hand, there is a case which ultimately led to victimization in human trafficking. What makes the difference—either a positive or a negative outcome—is dependent on whether the sense of community solidarity is mutually shared or not. In the village, if a needy family receives financial support from other community members, they can possibly avoid the worst outcome: the development of incidents into human trafficking. If, however, there is no support by the community, the circumstances in which they live will get worse, as in the cases of Sophia and Kuntiah. The existence of a system of mutual support in the village community can protect not only the human rights of the needy but also prevent the poor from falling into another trap of poverty. This support system also helps to decrease the possibility of human trafficking of persons in the village.

Meanwhile, the type of family which was made into the target of discrimination and prejudice is the one in isolation, with few contacts with the neighboring people. They are excluded from the community built on the basis of mutual support. As a result, they have to cope with every problem they have by themselves without financial and material—even consultative—support from the other members of the community. This situation makes it much harder and more severe for them, and they are so desperately in need that they are likely to become involved in human trafficking.

Vicious Spiral of Poverty—Isolation and the Sense of Disgrace

The life of Kuntiah was greatly affected by the rape incident which created a much worse situation. She said that her parents took it as "the disgrace of the family" and treated her coldly with more frequent violence against her. There were other cases of rape victims being abandoned by their families, and avoided or ignored by their close friends. Beneath such a negative attitude toward victims of sexual violence, there lies the sense of disgrace which is molded by the social norms and the gender code embraced in the society of Cambodia. A negative chain reaction, in other words, a vicious downward spiral, can be caused by factors inherent in the social structure of the rural villages in Cambodia.

The case of Kuntiah shows that a person in a socially weak position is more likely not only to be made into the target of discrimination and prejudice against poverty, sexual violence, and the deviation of the gender code but also isolation and alienation from the community. Exposure to structural violence makes needy people more vulnerable, so they can succumb to exploitation in the market economy, which will increase the risk of ending up in being traded in the human trafficking market.

DISCRIMINATION IN THE VILLAGE AND THE FEAR OF GOING BACK HOME

In general, victims of human trafficking originally from a village have a tendency to refrain from going back home. One of the reasons why they are reluctant to return is perhaps derived from the basic nature of the rural village in Cambodia. The rural village has two opposing characteristics: one is a positive system of mutual support among the community members, whereas the other is a tendency to oppress and exclude those who go against the traditional social norms. The latter is likely to be inflicted on trafficking victims in particular. The case of a fourteen-year-old girl called Rotah describes how she had to leave her home village because of too much suffering from the oppressive and exclusionary nature intrinsic to the rural village. She was a trafficking victim and in the end was helped out of it. After she returned to her village, she received discriminatory treatment from the villagers, who were filled with prejudice against her because she had been a trafficking victim, which she felt was undeserved. The details of her case illustrate how hard it is for a victim of human trafficking to get away from the exposure of structural violence.

Case Study: Rotah (fourteen years old)

Family Situation

Rotah's family consisted of her parents, brothers, and sisters. In total, there were five. The father was away from home as a migrant laborer, engaged in construction work. As part of their living expenses, the rest of the family counted on the money the father might send, but they had never received money from him, since he left home for work. So they sold their land and gained some cash for it. Afterward they had to move to different places. They managed to get by on some vegetables which were unsold in the market and by fishing. Nonetheless, they were always short of food. Rotah was told by her mother that she borrowed money to buy rice and daily commodities. Rotah and her siblings had never gone to school because they were constantly short of money.

Human Trafficking

One day someone visited Rotah's. He said that he lived in the same village, and they could come and talk to him when they needed help. He paid visits to them to try to get information about the real economic situation of the family. Each time he visited, he listened to them, knowing that they did not have enough money to live on. Gradually Rotah and the other family members built trust in him and saw him as a friend who was kind and good to them. On one day he visited, he suggested that some of them should go to Thailand for work, and they could earn somewhere between 10,000 and 50,000 baht. Suffering from a constant lack of income, the amount of money he described was so huge that they found the offer appealing. Rotah's mother decided to send her to Thailand for the job after she was told by the man that he would leave the necessary arrangement with someone he could trust. Once she got to Thailand, the man told Rotah's mother, she would know what to do and where to stay, yet he gave them no details. A "broker" completed all the preparations and procedures for crossing the border into Thailand.

During the middle of the night, they went through a jungle and crossed the border. When they exited the forest and arrived in Thailand a different "broker" who was supposed to take her to a brothel was waiting for them. On arriving at the brothel, she realized that she had been deceived and trafficked. She was ordered into prostitution every day from the evening and was forced to do housekeeping at the owner's house during the daytime. She was also sexually abused by the owner.

Going Back Home, and Discrimination and Prejudice

Just once Rotah was allowed to go back to her village accompanied by the broker. Her employer, the owner of the brothel, threatened her and strictly forbade her to talk about what had happened to her and where she had stayed. She was warned that if she talked to anybody about what happened to her, her family would have to pay the consequences. However, Rotah could not persevere and finally she told her mother about the situation she faced in Thailand. On listening to her daughter she was shocked and reported it to the police. Immediately after she went to the police the trafficker was arrested. Nevertheless, their neighbors came to know that Rotah had been in a brothel in Thailand, and they made discriminatory remarks about it. The villagers started to abuse her with the words that she was a girl raped by foreigners, or that she was a prostitute having sex for money. She was now avoided and ignored by those who had been friendly to her, and eventually so were her other family members.

Sometime later, a local NGO heard from the police that a human trafficking incident had occurred; so the NGO took measures to protect Rotah against this secondary damage as the target of discrimination and prejudice in the village. Rotah said that she wanted to go back home and stay with her family, but she could not do so because she was afraid of receiving personal attacks from the villagers about her past history. She was also afraid that the traffickers might come to kill her when they were let out of prison, and she had no idea when they would be released. Despite the fact that she was a victim of human trafficking, she blamed herself for being raped. She was discouraged, saying that she did not know what she could do for the future.

Isolation from Access to Mutual Support in a Community and Brokers—The Spiral of Fear

Rotah's family was isolated from the village and was also not allowed to participate in the small circle of solidarity built on the basis of mutual support and joined by a small number of neighboring persons. Just as in the case of Kuntiah, exclusionary treatment meant the loss of a safety net and a further step into poverty in a society where the cultural and social openness and awareness are low.

The direct cause of the human trafficking incident involving Rotah was the appearance of the trafficker just at the time when the family was alienated and isolated from the community. The trafficker paid frequent visits to Rotah's family in order to know how they made their living. With no close friend to rely on, Rotah took him as a friend who could help them with a caring intention. The trafficker said that she could earn much more money than she had ever had before if she found a job in Thailand. This gave them the hope that they would be able to get out of the vicious circle of poverty. However, the man whom she took as her friend was a trafficker.

It was when Rotah returned home once and told her mother about what had happened to her that the fact that she was in actuality trafficked was revealed. As far as the interviews collected by the author were concerned, the case of Rotah is quite exceptional: the victim lets the people around know what has happened to her. Unlike Rotah, generally victims of human trafficking are reluctant to talk about what has happened to them because they are intimidated by threats or violence from the business owners or employers. Another probable reason why they are unwilling to confide their personal matters to others is that they are afraid of receiving discriminatory remarks about them due to the prejudice against prostitutes. Rotah was still frightened that if the traffickers were let out of prison, they would come and kill her. Victims are threatened and are worried that the consequences of what they have done would be visited upon family members.

A girl of eleven trafficked to Thailand also said that she wanted to stay with her family if she could, but she did not really want to go back to the place she was originally from. If she went back there, she would be treated in an unfriendly manner because she was a prostitute and because her family remained poor. Other cases like hers show that trafficking victims in reality wanted to go back to their villages, but they were so afraid of being made the target of discriminatory and harsh remarks about their personal history as a prostitute that they give up going back home in the end.

The common reason why they hold back from going home probably comes from the oppressive and exclusionary nature inherent in the rural Cambodian villages, where victims of human trafficking would fear discrimination and prejudice toward anyone who has gone against the traditional social norms. This feeling of fear of isolation makes them unwilling to return to their home, and this increases the risk of secondary trafficking in persons. In this sense, it is necessary to bear in mind that the protective measures taken for victims and their families do not always turn the situation for the better but often have the reverse effect of turning circumstances for the worse.

The Consciousness of Guilt in Victims of Human Trafficking

In the narrow and closed society of the rural village, the alienation of victims of trafficking and their families has had a great influence on the development

Discriminated and Isolated, a Family Lives in the Back of the Community. *Source*: ©Yuko Shimazaki.

of the consciousness of guilt in victims themselves. In general, victims tend to blame themselves for all of the causes of having been trafficked because they feel guilty about being deceived into sex trafficking—a situation against the social norms and the gender code. This way of thinking possibly comes from the fact that they were exposed to severe criticism from their neighbors when they returned home, which then caused them to be isolated from the villages of their origin.

Rotah repeatedly said that she hated herself, having been ashamed of her past history of being trafficked to a brothel, thinking that she fell into disgrace. Situations such as this cause victims to fall into despair so often that they hurt themselves or attempt suicide after they are accommodated in a shelter.

Vocational programs for the purpose of sending trafficking victims back home in a safer way are developed and offered by many NGOs and international organizations. However, some organizations focus so much effort on sending victims back home that they have not sufficiently considered what going back home could mean for the victims. For this reason, sometimes their support might generate reverse consequences. Thus, it is necessary to carefully watch what they provide to victims as part of supporting program.

Of great importance in working on human trafficking issues are the establishment and the arrangement of a safety net so that vulnerable families and victims of trafficking won't fall through. At the same time, it is necessary to raise the awareness of members of rural villages so that discrimination and prejudice against human trafficking victims are reduced to the lowest possible level. This not only encourages the protection of victims against isolation from the village caused by the discriminatory attitudes of the villagers but also helps to prevent them from getting involved in secondary trafficking and falling into further poverty. Consequently, such efforts lead to offering victims and the vulnerable the opportunity to achieve their economic independence, by creating self-confidence.

SUMMARY

Considering the Rural Village from the Viewpoint of a Trafficked Victim

This chapter focuses on three cases to consider the process in which human trafficking incidents occur and the actual situation of secondary victimization in the rural village. Each of the three families went through the separation of family brought about by migrant labor and domestic violence, and the series of these events ended up with a member of the family becoming the victim of human trafficking. They suffered from the negative effects of structural violence intrinsic to the society in which they lived and from oppression inflicted by the traditional social norms embraced in the rural villages of Cambodia. By these factors they were hampered from trying to make their living conditions better. Indeed, they were in a situation that made it more difficult for them to take a step forward to change their lives for the better.

The closed society of rural villages where human relationships have already been fixed tends to refuse to accept victims of human trafficking and labels them as people who have gone against the social norms and the gender code. That is why the victims themselves are so reluctant to go back to the villages of their origin and, in the end, give up. From this perspective, it is necessary for the villages to offer a safer place where they can live without being intimidated of receiving criticism of their personal history. Furthermore, it is desirable for the villages to be able to provide them with support in achieving their independence with continuous care. Yet, in many cases, the village itself is actually a hotbed of secondary damage such as discrimination, prejudice, and the violation of the human rights of victims of human trafficking.

These circumstances are created by the combination of multiple causes such as structural violence, authoritarianism inherent in the society of Cambodia, and its cultural norms. The society of Cambodia forms a hierarchy, which embraces just a few economic haves on top and the needy making up the majority at the bottom. Because of this social structure, with a wide economic gap between haves and have-nots, discrimination against the poor and the vulnerable and the violation of their human rights are still important issues for today's Cambodia in the sense that these problems are highly likely to bring about another vicious spiral of poverty. The incidence of human trafficking in the rural villages in Cambodia has to be studied carefully not only from the viewpoint of the social structure behind the individual cases, but also from that of its cultural norms.

NOTES

1. Then one dollar was calculated at 4,000 riel in rural village. Riel is Cambodian currency.

2. Baht is the Thai currency.

3. Even though the neighbors were willing to offer their cooperation for investigation, the victims themselves had mixed feelings. Despite the fact that there was neither criticism nor gossip circulated about them, they developed an acute fear that they had deviated from the gender code accepted in Cambodia, and felt deeply ashamed of it. These are supported by the remarks of the victims interviewed thus: "My grandfather had been good to me, but he started to take a cold attitude toward me"; and "when I go back home, I am afraid that I might be criticized as a raped woman" (when interviewed, she was accommodated in a shelter).

Chapter 2

Victims of Human Trafficking along the Cambodian–Thai Border

Who Are They?

This chapter attempts to consider the actual situation created by the negative circle of poverty: how difficult it is to break away from poverty, once the people of a socially vulnerable group fall into its trap. This subject is going to be discussed in terms of how and why transnational human trafficking occurs, and also in what way persons are involved in the system of commercial trading in humans, with several examples cited.

POIPET: THE BORDER AREA

Poipet (Paoy Paet, ប៉ោយប៉ែត) belongs to the province of Banteay Meanchey in the north of Cambodia. It is also close to the border with Thailand, Aranyaprathet in the province of Sa Kaeo. Looking back to the history of Cambodia during the period 1979–1993, several refugee camps were set up in the areas close to the Cambodian–Thai borders after the collapse of the Pol Pot regime.

Except for the camp in Khao-I-Dang, other camps in the border area, under political intervention and the stationing of anti-government soldiers, were taken over as military bases. In general, the office of the UN High Commissioner for Refugees (UNHCR) had the authority to protect refugees accommodated in the camps and help them to resettle to third countries.

However, instead of the UNHCR, the UN Border Relief Operation (UNBRO) temporarily extended emergency support to the displaced persons who fled to the camps other than Khao-I-Dang. The UNBRO was an organization set up in 1982 without definable authority to provide humane protection for refugees. Eventually, those who were accommodated in the camps but for Khao-I-Dang were regarded as Internally Displaced Persons (IDPs). UNBRO took these IDPs under its protection.[1] In 1992 when returning refugees to their home villages was carried out, more than 350,000 persons crowded in the area close to the border between Cambodia and Thailand.[2]

After the return of refugees to their villages, the people who lost the place to live surged ahead to Poipet.[3] Following the closure of refugee camps, supporting organizations prepared places for their resettlement in Poipet. The space is not large enough for farming but just for building living accommodations. Its landscape offers no impression as a pastoral village, only just the place to live.

Subsequently, encouraged by a favorable wind from the growth of the domestic economy, Poipet took on importance in the exchange of people and goods, boasting a brisk and flourishing trade between Cambodia and Thailand. This attracted many people looking for a job from all parts of Cambodia. In Poipet, there is a market called Rong Klua, which is a good source of employment. This is an enormous market which stretches over both the countries of Cambodia and Thailand. The jobs typical of Poipet are a carrier of cart for a small amount of things; work in the border casino; and work in the factories gathered on the side of Cambodia. In coming and going between the two countries while working in the market, Cambodians pay for a border ticket for crossing the border for daily workers.

At present, Poipet plays an important part not only as the foothold of the southern economic corridor within the Greater Mekong Subregion (GMS), but also as a transit place to the world market. GMS is a form of regional economic cooperative, aiming for brisk economic activity among the nations concerned. In addition, Poipet was designated as a Special Economic Zone (SEZ) in Cambodia. Within the economic zone, companies with foreign capital affiliation are legally privileged. As the result of this system, foreign affiliates increased, and it led to the creation of employment. Thus, the availability of job openings attracted many migrant workers from distant parts of the country.

Cambodian workers migrated to Poipet, looking for a job in the expectation of making their living better. However, as a majority of them are from among the poorest without special skills, engagement in physical labor is the only choice they can make. Even though they cross the border and go to Thailand where the general wage level is higher than that in Cambodia, they can probably only earn the same amount of money as the minimum wage of Cambodia. In this sense, the actual working conditions fall short of their expectations, and not all migrants in Poipet are successful.

The Cambodian-Thai Border. People Waiting for the Opening of the Gate. In the Early Morning There Is a Long Line. *Source*: ©Yuko Shimazaki.

People Carrying Things by Drawing a Cart at the Border. *Source*: ©Yuko Shimazaki.

THE TYPES OF PEOPLE IN POIPET

The Overview of the Researched Area

A survey including interviews was conducted in Village A and Village B, both of which showed extremely high incidences of human trafficking.[4] Characteristics of those village were that the majority of residents were poor, the mobility of their populations was intense, and peace was unstable.[5] The villages mainly consisted of families of returnees and displaced persons, and those of migrant workers. According to the NGO staff, during one year in 2006, the number of women and girls victimized by human trafficking was as follows: in Village A, there were four cases, and two cases were attempted. As for the Village B, there were seven cases. According to a staff member of an NGO, "this is just the tip of iceberg."[6] These victims were only the ones eventually taken care of by NGOs, so in fact there were probably more unreported victims.

The Background of Village A

Village A was constructed in 1998 as a part of the resettlement of refugees. Priority was given to families with tight living conditions, those with many children to be raised, and those families without a father. The majority of the residents in Village A used to make their living by begging and had neither a house nor a job. A resident knowing the situation then said that gambling and the use of drugs was a familiar sight in the village. Many people came to Village A from various rural parts of Cambodia. With its closeness to the border with Thailand, the mobility of people was active. Migrant workers from other provinces grew gradually in number, and eventually the buying and selling of land was put into practice among residents.

The Background of Village B

Village B is a comparatively newly built community, made up of seasonal migratory workers and migrant families from rural villages. In general, every house in the village was already built and was available for rent. Sitting tenants had to pay 15 baht (Thai currency) a day for rent (the rental fee at the time this research was conducted). In principle, if a tenant failed to pay 15 baht by the due date, they had to leave the house. According to a resident in the village, in the past they did not have to pay for the rent, but some time ago people identifying themselves as the landowner or the landlord came to the village from Phnom Penh and started to collect rent for the houses from the residents.

As a whole, the houses in Village B were similarly built of wood in a platform style. In some houses, the outer walls were made of bamboo or tinplate. In others, they were covered by newspapers or plastic sheets. Some houses had no cover on the outer wall, like a stairwell style house. In many houses, the floor was so dilapidated that the ground was seen through it.

There were many people out of work then in the village. In addition, there was a rumor that went around the village that illicit dealers of narcotic drugs and stimulant drugs were active. Because of the situation, the residents were on the watch for others and tried not to meddle in other people's business. One woman interviewed then said that her husband would not tell her what kind of job he was engaged in.[7] Fifteen days before the interview was taken, someone she had never met came to see her husband and took him away somewhere. Since then, her husband had never come back home. She wondered if he might have been involved in drug trafficking.

The Categorization of the Residents and the Family Situation

The residents in the areas researched are categorized as: refugees and displaced persons from the camps; families who came to Poipet immediately after the Cambodian Civil War; women with personal reasons, for example, a single parent and her children or victims of domestic violence; those who had no alternative but to migrate to Poipet because, for instance, of tight economic conditions, having no land property, discrimination and prejudice; migratory laborers temporarily staying for the purpose of earning income; migrants who had sold their land before they moved to Poipet.

There was great variety in the makeup of families: parents and children; siblings only; grandparents and grandchildren; aunts and uncles, living with their nieces and nephews; a single parent and children; and single women sharing a house. Such variety is one of the features typical of Poipet.

Except for persons out of work, the means of the villagers' livelihood are: carrying things in a cart drawn by a person; construction; daywork in the market; laundry; begging; selling things on the street; manufacturing; breeding hogs (daily work for someone else); housekeeping; interpretation; and finally, the services in the casino. Despite the fact that a variety of job openings in Poipet attract migrants from other parts of Cambodia, people find it difficult to get a job, contrary to their expectations.

Usually workers get wages on a daily basis and the payment is approximately 100 baht on average (the amount at the time this research was conducted), with the exception of higher-paying jobs such as interpretation. In actuality, the average income of 100 baht per day, cited above, is lower than the minimum wage, 140 baht in Payao, northern Thailand (researched in 2006).[8] In other words, even if Cambodian workers get a job in Thailand, the wage paid to them does not meet the legal standard. As they had to buy not only food but everything they needed in cash, they described the way they lived as living from hand to mouth or living day by day with almost no money left.

In recent years, Village B was designated as a SEZ, and this seemed to create an economic income gap between the residents. This can be defined as an inequality between workers without education and special vocational skills and migrants from rural villages intending to stay in Poipet for a short time. In particular, for the poor and vulnerable, there is no other course but to be engaged in work which would be considered at least close to illegal. Under these circumstances, they have to work for the payment, even though this is less than the minimum wage. Still, not all the workers in Poipet are the poorest—some workers make use of their skills and previous vocational experience. Yet, the most socially vulnerable without education and skills are highly likely to be exposed to the risks of being trafficked.

Neighboring Relations between Residents

After a survey including interviews conducted in Village A and Village B, it was found that the residents of both villages showed a tendency to form an unsociable neighborhood. When the interviews were collected from the residents concerned, they answered thus: "They were so busy with their own business that they had no chance to care about others"; "they had almost no personal information about others, who they were or where they came from, so they tried not to be in touch"; and "they had almost no chance of getting to know each other, as people always came and went."

Typical social problems in the neighborhoods were: domestic violence (twelve cases); troubles with their neighbors (eight); drug dependence (two); alcoholic dependence (two); and child abuse (five). The total answers are thirty-nine with multiple answers possible. A resident mentioned that "angry shouting had already become a familiar sight." A village leader also said disappointedly that "children in the village had already gotten used to the sight of violence in the neighborhood, such as family violence."

In Poipet, international organizations and NGOs have extended support to and protection for needy people, homeless people, refugees, and trafficked persons in returning them to their home villages. They also have been actively engaged in educational aid and in offering shelter to migratory workers who were forcibly repatriated. Nonetheless, as far as the present situation is concerned, unfortunately it seems that these supporting measures failed to bring about a lasting effect on the residents.

Former Refugees and Poverty

Returning refugees and displaced persons to their home villages from the border camp was carried out under the control of the United Nations High Commissioner for Refugees. There are problems with poverty among the

Migrating Workers' Houses. *Source*: ©Yuko Shimazaki.

Houses in a Remote Place.

returnees living in Village A. Some had neither family members nor relatives and lived on the street without a place to go back to. Others lost their land because of redistribution. There were also those who could not go back home for the sake of safety, because landmines were placed on or under the ground. These are the people who still have enormous difficulties in emerging from poverty.

According to the results from the survey in Poipet, twelve families out of twenty-five are returnees from the border camp, and at present they gain a living through migrant labor. They passed through the refugee camp in the border area, and their personal background was deeply connected with the history of the Cambodian Civil War. The present situation in which they live and in what way they are involved in human trafficking is examined with a presentation of actual cases collected from the interviews.

The Victimization from Human Trafficking in the Families of Former Refugees: Case Study

Manet (seventeen years old)
At present, Manet lives with her mother, and elder and younger sisters

From the Camp in the Border Area to Poipet

After leaving the camp in the border area, Manet's parents were homeless and lived in one place or another. When begging on the street, her parents heard by chance that they would be given a house by an NGO so they moved to Village A. Although they received a house they still had no means of gaining food. Thus, their life did not turn for the better. In Village A external supporting organizations had extended aid to the residents in rebuilding their lives for several years. After these organizations pulled out of the village, Manet's family needed to earn a livelihood independently. Manet's father was out of work, and he became dependent on alcohol. He started to commit acts of violence against his wife and daughters.

The Living Conditions of Her Family

Manet's elder sister made a living by drawing a cart to carry things. Nonetheless, it was not enough for the whole family to live on. They had to borrow money to make up for the shortage. They were unable to borrow money from a moneylender because they had no article like a television set or motorbike to pawn or use as collateral. For this reason, they borrowed money from their acquaintances with the promise that Manet's elder sister working in Thailand would pay back the money. Consequently, their debts kept mounting.

They had one meal a day, and for drinking they boiled well water. Manet and her sisters had never been to school. Manet was sick in bed for many days, but she could not afford to pay for her medical treatment and medicine. In the neighborhood, drug trafficking, fights between gangs, and thefts occurred regularly, so she would not go out, especially at night.

The Victimization of Manet in Human Trafficking

Before she became a human trafficking victim, Manet used to make a living by drawing a cart to carry things along the Cambodian–Thai borders, and sometimes did laundry in the village. However, it was difficult for her to support her family. Her parents were physically weak and their health did not allow them to work. Instead, fifteen-year-old Manet went over to the market on the Thai side of the border, looking for a broker who could possibly get her a job. A Thai broker approached her about a job opening, saying that if she worked in Thailand as a waitress, she could earn as much as 5,000 baht a month. Manet told her mother that she would like to take the job offer. Anxious about her daughter, the mother told her that working in Thailand seemed quite dangerous. Naturally, the mother disagreed with her. Nonetheless, Manet believed that it should be all right for her to accept the offer on the grounds that many people so far had been to Thailand as migrant workers. Eventually, Manet made up her mind to go to Thailand for the sake of her family whose economic condition was extremely tight at that time. However, in fact, the place where she was supposed to work was not a restaurant in Thailand but a brothel in Malaysia.

Manet Came Back to Village A and Was Victimized Again

One day Manet ran out of the brothel. When standing on the street alone, Manet was taken into protective custody by the Malaysian Police. After six months of custody, she came back to Cambodia. Then she was put in protection by an NGO, and she went back to Village A. When she arrived in the village, the neighboring people came to know that she had been in a brothel. As the village itself had many transients who held only tenuous relationships, the gossip that she had been in a brothel did not circulate rapidly. Nonetheless, she decided to leave Village A so as to avoid attracting attention in case the gossip that she was a prostitute should incite discrimination against her. In the village where she started her life anew, it was difficult for her to find a job. Again she went over to the market on the Thai side and asked a broker she knew to get her a job. The broker told her that she could earn 2,000 baht a month in a restaurant in Thailand. Again she believed what the broker said to her. Then she was accompanied by the broker to Thailand. According to her, "it never occurred to her that she would be deceived again, because the broker was not a total stranger but someone she knew." Yet, the place she was taken to was a brothel in the center of Thailand. It was not a restaurant as she was told beforehand. Manet was bitterly disappointed at another disheartening experience. In addition to being forced into prostitution, she was also sexually victimized by the owner of the brothel. Since then, she felt something unusual in her health, and occasionally she suffered from stomachaches, headaches, or a slight fever. When she finally told the owner of the brothel that she was poor in health, she was allowed to go back to Cambodia. Then a Thai broker accompanied her and left her at the border between Cambodia and Thailand. While she was alone near the border, she was stopped and questioned by the Cambodian border guards. The border police made contact with a supporting organization, which gave her protection. Now she said that "she was ill with difficulties in breathing."

The Actual Living Situation of a Family of Former Refugees and Human Trafficking

Manet's parents lived on the street after they left the refugee camp, making their living by begging. Their household was quite unstable because they lived from day to day without any definite objective. They heard by chance that if they moved to Village A parcel of land would be given to them. For this reason, they decided to migrate, although they had no specific or concrete perspective on how to make a livelihood for the future.

As a whole, there is a tendency for returnees to be clearly dependent upon others. For instance, when interviewed, some returnees answered that "they expected supporting organizations to help them out of their tight economic situation"; and when they encountered difficulties, "NGOs or organizations would surely come again and help them." Remarkable is the lack of awareness of self-help in their attitude toward how to make a livelihood. For example, there were answers such as "their children were supposed to look after their parents"; "their daughters should go to work and earn money"; and "they could count on NGOs to help them." In short, they tend to show passivity in improving their lives.

Because of her health condition, Manet's mother was not able to work (her father had, by then, disappeared). For her mother, the three daughters—Manet and her elder and younger sisters—had to take responsibility for earning money for the family's sake. Manet went over to the Thai side of the market and made contact with a broker. Indeed, this was the very beginning of her victimization through human trafficking. According to her, brokers came to the village quite often. She had heard that they perpetrated sexual violence on women in the village and committed fraud upon villagers.

That is the reason why she went over to Thailand, looking for someone she could trust.

In the case of human trafficking occurring in the area close to the border with Thailand, as a tendency, victims voluntarily make contact with brokers and take job offers. On the contrary, in rural villages brokers themselves look for targets and make direct approaches with a job proposal. When a decision is made, in many cases, pressure is brought on victims to migrate in order to live up to the expectations of their parents, relations, or persons they know.

Poipet attracts not only job seekers but also brokers, just like a magnet. It is an economic staging area because geographically it has good access to the Thai market, which has connections with other markets worldwide. Because the Thai market provides employment, brokers come to Poipet to meet the demand. Commercial trade in persons is not limited within Cambodia but victims are taken to such neighboring countries as Thailand, Malaysia, and Indonesia. The case of Manet shows how the network of human trafficking is developed internationally.

After she was taken into protective custody by the Malaysian Police, Manet came back to Cambodia. Compared to conditions in more rural parts of the country, she felt less prejudice against prostitution when she came back to her home village. In addition, she found that the gossip about her personal experience in a brothel in Malaysia did not spread as wide and quickly as it would have in a rural village. Nonetheless, an NGO advised her not to attract attention so as to avoid secondary damage. Taking up the advice, she moved to a different place. In the place where she started anew, she approached voluntarily another broker because she wanted to get a job for her own livelihood. Unfortunately, again she was trafficked and ended up being sold to a brothel in Thailand this time. Even though she was fully aware of risks, she was in a situation in which she had no other alternative but to migrate for her own living.

When she was asked the question of whether she thought of deception again, Manet answered that "the broker she talked to was someone she had met before, so the thought of being deceived had never occurred to her." As a whole, victims trafficked in the border area tend to describe the brokers they talked to as "someone they know" or "someone they have met before." In actuality, there is perception gap between people in a rural village and those living in a border village about the meaning of "an acquaintance." In interviews with victims trafficked in a border village, to the question of what extent they knew the people they described as "acquaintances," they explained thus: "a person from whom they had bought fruit before" and "a person with whom they had talked several times in the market before." It can be inferred that human relationships themselves are formed from casual acquaintances in a border village because of the transient nature of the people who live there.

The Family of the Former Refugees and the Social Structure

Like a magnet, the area close to the border with Thailand is a place that attracts needy people and families who look for jobs. The family of Manet was one of these, and had lived there for a long period of time. They tried to improve their living situation, but still they were in chronic poverty. In this area, a structure of domination and subordination between brokers and trafficked victims exists. On one hand, brokers enjoy supremacy over their targets in the sense that it is brokers who can provide them with a job. On the other hand, these victims are put in a vulnerable position because they think that it is only the brokers whom they can depend on. Accidentally, Manet slipped into this structure. People in a socially weaker position are most likely to be deprived of their human dignity and autonomy in their own lives by structural violence. These vulnerable people can be easily controlled by social groups with power and authority.

More than two decades have already passed since refugees of the Cambodian Civil War returned to their home villages. However, even now many of them are still faced with formidable difficulties in stopping the negative spiral of poverty. This demonstrates that the needy are forced to remain

Manet. *Source*: ©Yuko Shimazaki.

at the lowest level of the social hierarchy. Anytime and anywhere, human society invariably produces marginal groups and includes them within its structure. Inevitably, the weak must be subordinate to the strong. In this way, poverty is reproduced as long as society maintains the relationship between subordinates and superiors. To sum up, such social structure in itself is violent against the weak, and these vulnerable people are destined to become more vulnerable than ever.

THE NEGATIVE SPIRAL TRAP AND THE MIGRANT FAMILY

The area close to the border with Thailand has the advantage that it is comparatively easier for people to find jobs. Meanwhile, unlike life in the rural village, it requires residents to buy everything they need in cash; so they are always conscious of the importance of earning cash. Although they are fully aware of various risks, day laborers will cross the border to be engaged in a job. However, crossing the border through unofficial routes often requires that a bribe has to be given to the border police or brokers.

Migrants come to Poipet with the hope of improving their lives economically. However, in fact, some migratory workers encounter a reality that is widely different from the one they expected, and some of them can become addicted to alcohol or gambling to escape the situation they are faced with. Poipet is deeply engaged in human trafficking: out of fifty interviewed trafficked victims, thirteen were its residents, and nine came to Poipet as either a transit place or as the final destination of trafficking. Although human trafficking occurs across the whole of Cambodia, in comparison, the frequency of human trafficking in Poipet is greater.

This is partly because, with its economic prosperity, Thailand plays an important role as the economic center of Southeast Asia. Southeast Asia is considered to be one of the most promising actors in the world economy. Its economic growth makes it possible to afford an abundant supply of labor. Thus, it attracts various brokers, and among them, traffickers are surely included. Job seekers migrate to Poipet, and generally they become engaged in physical labor. In many cases, physical labor is work done on a daily wage basis, and so it is insecure in terms of employment. It can be said that, in fact, it is these manual laborers who have laid the foundation of the present economic growth and prosperity of Southeast Asia. By taking up an actual case of a victimized family living in Poipet, why and how a migratory family became involved in human trafficking is going to be considered.

The Mother-Child Family and Human Trafficking—Living Environment Producing Victims of Human Trafficking: Case Study

Niam (forty-three years old)
living with her nine-year-old daughter

Why and How Niam Moved to Poipet and Her Living Situation

Niam was a victim of violence from her husband and mother-in-law before she moved to Poipet. She could not bear the pain of domestic violence any longer, so she ran away from them, taking her daughters with her. That is why she came to Poipet. Her parents and siblings were killed in the Cambodian Civil War. She had relatives, but she was out of touch with them. She met a man in Poipet and started to live with him. He was unemployed, and when he got drunk, he hit her on the head with a stone. Although she went to the police seeking protection against his violence, there was no improvement in the situation. When he knew that Niam asked for help from the police, he got angry and it drove him to further violence. Niam was so ashamed of her victimization that she simply could not speak about it to anyone in the neighborhood. His violence got worse and worse, and even in front of her children he behaved violently toward her on a daily basis. When she was hit on the head by him, Niam needed surgery. As she had no cash with which to pay for her medical treatment, she had to sell the land she had owned. The cash she gained by selling the land was spent on her surgery and debt repayments. At that time, the man left her and started to live with another woman.

As she had already parted with the land she owned at that point, she had to look for a place to live somewhere. Finally, she found a house with a room, small in size. Its tinplate roof was made so poorly that the rain came in when it was windy. The front door did not close properly. In addition, the sewage did not drain properly and gave off a bad smell. Although it was an insecure and unsanitary place to live, it was the only one choice she could make.

The Victimization of Her Daughter in Human Trafficking

Four months before she was interviewed, an acquaintance living in the same village paid a visit to Niam. The visitor was a woman, who later was found to be a trafficker, and she asked Niam to let her have Niam's two-year-old daughter for begging in Thailand. In other words, she made an approach to Niam to ask for "child rental," which makes children play a child's part beside a beggar in pretending to be a family or a parent and a child. The "rental period" was supposed to be a month. Then Niam was offered the payment of 1,000 baht as "rental fee." The woman said that surely her daughter would be looked after and fed well. Niam wondered if she could trust the offer and felt suspicious of it, but she finally gave in. When she thought of difficulties of feeding her children every day, she desperately needed money. She had no one to ask for advice around her, so she had to take a decision about her daughter's situation. Afterward, the woman "acquaintance" made all the necessary preparations for taking Niam's daughter to Thailand.

However, Niam did not receive the promised 1,000 baht for the "rental charge" of her daughter. Even after three months had passed (when the interview with her was undertaken, her daughter had already been missing for three months), her daughter had never come back to her. Now that she had become extremely and acutely worried about her daughter, Niam asked the woman's son about the situation. However, he only said that he knew nothing about it, and Niam was finally paid 1,500 baht in cash. She pressed the woman to bring her daughter back to her. Since then the woman had never appeared before Niam.

Niam was desperate to know whether her daughter was really taken to Thailand and whether she was still alive or not. Even when she tried to get information about her daughter out of him, the son of the "broker" just said he knew nothing about her daughter and would not say more. Niam bitterly regretted what she had done with her daughter, and she absolutely thought that she should not have left her daughter with the "broker."

Even worse, another broker paid frequent visits to Niam and approached her for a fresh "child rental" of her nine-year-old daughter, saying that she could earn 2,000 baht a month by begging in Thailand. However, Niam declared in a determined way and with tears in her eyes that she would never send her daughter away to Thailand.

Women and Poverty

Behind Niam's migration to Poipet was the motivation to flee from family violence. In Cambodia, it is a social and cultural custom for a husband to live with the family of his wife (uxorilocal residence and matriliny). In Niam's case, however, her parents had died during the Cambodian Civil War, so she lived with her husband's family. Unfortunately, she found it difficult to keep good terms with her mother-in-law, who behaved violently toward her. Thus, she escaped the violence inflicted by her husband's family on her.

Despite the fact that she moved to Poipet with her daughters, seeking a peaceful life, again she had to spend every day frightened of violence against her from the man she lived with. Niam confessed that she, too, had used violence against her children because she saw the man whom she lived with behaving violently in front of her children on a daily basis. Given this was the case, it would seem like a negative chain reaction of violence, where an abused person turns into an abuser on a weaker family member, probably derived from domestic power structure.

In general, in the area close to the border with Thailand, those who seek jobs make contact with brokers voluntarily, asking for a job opening. However, in Niam's case, a broker personally made an approach with the intention of making her daughter into a target of trafficking. From the perspective of the broker, the two-year-old girl was a valuable commercial item, because trafficking in children is much more profitable when the targets are younger.

According to what Niam said, the broker prepared documents, taking a picture of her daughter. When these documents were shown to her, Niam could not grasp what they meant, because she was illiterate. The broker just said that these were the documents necessary to take the girl to Thailand. Then a question arises: "Is Niam an offender who sold her daughter, or is she a victim whose daughter was trafficked?" In order to get a better understanding of what human trafficking is, it is important to consider the social structure and the living conditions of a trafficked victim and their family members.

The viewpoints providing footholds for problems with human trafficking are the following: What creates vulnerable groups in society?; What influences are exerted on them?; and Why and how these people are involved in human trafficking? in particular, the family of the mother and children.

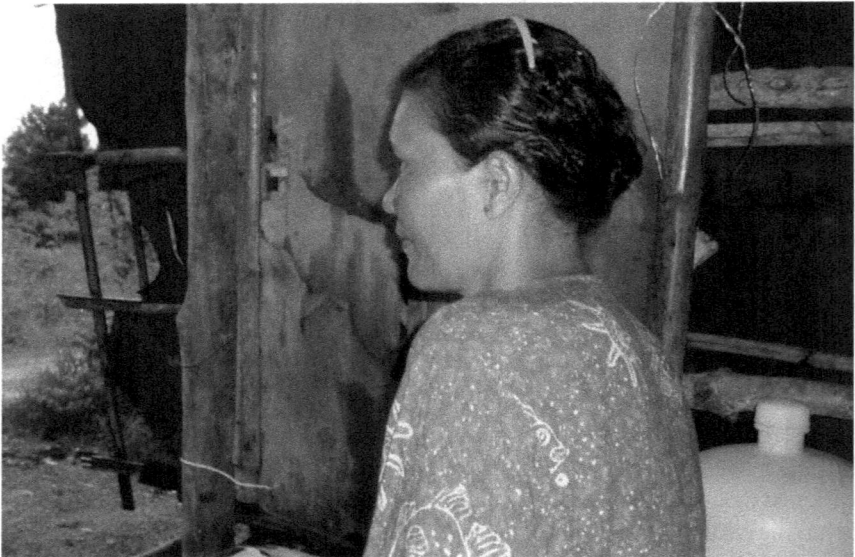

Niam. *Source*: ©Yuko Shimazaki.

The Family without Land Property and Human Trafficking: Case Study

Sreymon (fourteen years old)
The family situation: her parents, five brothers, and two sisters

The Motivation of Her Migration to Poipet

Sreymon's family sold their land, thereby gaining cash for the father's medical treatment and their living expenses. After that, they became homeless and lived in different places, sometimes staying at their relatives' place, and other times at a temple. While looking for a job, Sreymon's family moved to Siem Reap, but against their expectations, they were unable to find a job. Then a person told them that possibly they could get a job if they went to Poipet. That is why the family of Sreymon moved to Poipet.

In Poipet, Sreymon's mother, and her brothers and sisters sold fruit and coconuts. Her father, a former soldier, was in fragile health, so it was difficult for him to find fixed employment. Only when he was in good health, he was engaged in carrying things in a bicycle-drawn cart and earned about 80 baht a day.

The Victimization of Sreymon in Human Trafficking

Sreymon found a job after her mother borrowed money from her acquaintance and paid the brokerage fee. The broker would not tell her about the details of her job, but just said that she would know where to work and what to do when she arrived in Thailand. She was also told that she could never fail to earn money if only she were to go to Thailand. Still, the details were kept untold. She was accompanied by the broker and arrived in Pattaya, but at first she was unable to identify where she was. The broker had already been paid by an employer in Pattaya, and it was only when she arrived in Pattaya that Sreymon realized she had been trafficked. She had no idea how much money was paid for her trafficking. In Pattaya, she was ordered to beg for money on the street during the day. From 4 o'clock in the evening till dawn, she was forced into prostitution at a brothel. While begging on the street, she was kept under observation.

(When interviewed, she was under protection.)

Migration Done Out of Necessity, Not of Choice

The poverty of Sreymon's family was aggravated in no time after they parted with their land. Being homeless, they had to frequently change their place to live within the village. In the rural village where discrimination and prejudice against the poor and needy are displayed overtly, the family of Sreymon was discriminated against because their poverty deepened. As a result, they dropped down to the bottom of the social hierarchy. In rural villages, generally human relationships are arranged in different levels of social importance from highest to lowest, and these are fixed. Thus, once a family is excluded from the social hierarchical order they will lose membership in the community. Sreymon's family was not considered to be a member of the village any longer. Marginalized in the village, they decided to migrate to Siem Reap to find work. There was no other alternative for them but to leave the village for Siem Reap. Taking the migration by Sreymon's family into consideration, a question arises: Can migration done out of necessity really be regarded as voluntary in a strict sense?

The movement of people can be divided into two categories: involuntary migration (forced migration) and voluntary migration. The former refers to refugees and displaced persons who are forced to leave their country or home because of war or the outbreak of a natural disaster or for political, religious, or social reasons. The latter is applied to those who go and live or work in another country, regardless of the internal situation of their country, but for personal reasons, especially for economic reasons.

In a way the migration by the family of Sreymon appears to be a voluntary one. Seemingly they made the decision to migrate to Siem Reap by themselves because they wanted to escape from discrimination and marginalization on the grounds of their poverty. Behind the personal reason for their migration, there probably was a situation which forced migration upon them. Ostensibly they set out for migration voluntarily; however, it can be considered involuntary migration because they were pushed into making the decision by such external factors as poverty, discrimination, and social exclusion. Therefore, in deciding to migrate, personal reasons and social reasons are closely connected with each other. In fact, there are quite a few Cambodian migratory workers forced into migration by such social factors, with no other alternatives available.

In order to grasp the actual situation of the migrant workers in the border area, it is vitally necessary to observe the social circumstances of those who make the decision to migrate, and why and how they reach the border area. Usually, NGOs and supporting organizations extend aid to families arriving at the border with the view of sending them back to the rural villages they originally come from. However, aid and support in view of returning them to their villages is probably inadequate.

The reason for the insufficiency is that these people had no other alternative available than migration, and they finally came to Poipet in expectation of finding a job, in desperate need of making their own living. In other words, they are the people pushed into migration by certain social factors, such as discrimination, prejudice, and social exclusion on the grounds of their poverty. Therefore, even if they eventually go back home, they are likely to face discrimination, prejudice, and marginalization again, exactly the same situation as they used to endure. That is why sending them back to their home villages may not necessarily be a solution to the problems they have.

Invisible Perpetrators—Brokers of Human Trafficking

In Poipet, Sreymon got a job after her mother paid the brokerage fee to a broker. This so-called acquaintance sometimes visited Village B where Sreymon's family lived. Poipet functions as a place where day laborers come together to obtain work for the day. Unlike farm work requiring steady care and effort, this is an environment in which work done on a daily basis is the main source of income in cash. Thus, brokers are essential for migratory workers.

In reality, not all brokers are honest—some are agents acting for human trafficking. Looking at the case of Sreymon, she was accompanied by a broker she knew to a brothel in Pattaya. In fact, the broker who received the brokerage fee was a trafficker from the very beginning. It is generally quite difficult for trafficked victims to identify the trafficker, and when and where they were traded. According to other victims who were trafficked and taken to a brothel, they didn't think that the brokers who got them the job were traffickers, nor did the idea of being deceived occur to them. The victims were incapable of differentiating between honest brokers and traffickers. From these accounts it's clear that regular brokers and traffickers are intermingled in Poipet. In other words, there are quite a few traffickers who pass by the name of "brokers." These "invisible offenders" play an active role in connecting trafficked victims with the labor market behind the scenes.

Women Migrant Workers Leaving Their Family behind and Human Trafficking: Case Study

Chariya (twenty-four years old)

The Living Situation of Chariya before Her Migration to Poipet

Chariya was the breadwinner of the family because her parents and younger sister were physically weak and were not able to work. Brought up in a needy family, neither Chariya nor her sister had ever been to school. As they lived in tight living conditions, Chariya was told by her father to earn money in Poipet. For the sake of her family's economic improvement, she made the decision to migrate to Poipet.

The Situation with Which Chariya Was Faced in Poipet

When she came to Poipet, she was a day laborer engaged in farm work on the Thailand side of the border. The work was paid at a rate of about 130,000 riel (approximately US$30-32) per hectare, and it was shared among five people, including her. She said that she could not earn as she expected. Life in Poipet required a lot of money because she had to buy everything in cash. She became pregnant after being raped by a man she met during her migration.

When she went back home and told her parents that she was pregnant, Chariya was treated coldly, particularly by her mother. As her premarital pregnancy brought disgrace on family, she was abandoned by them. Then she felt ashamed of the treatment she was given by her family. Even though she was pregnant and did not know where to go, she thought she had better leave the village for Poipet again, where probably there were more job openings than in other places. This is the only one thing she could do for her situation. When she made contact with a broker again, she was told that there was a job in a restaurant somewhere in Cambodia. Then she was accompanied by the broker to another province. While she was pregnant, the place she was sent to was not a restaurant but a brothel. She was taken into protective custody by the police at the brothel and sent to a shelter of an NGO (when interviewed, she was under protection).

On Returning to the Village of Her Own

Chariya said that she wanted to go back home and stay with her family, but she could not. This is because she was afraid of being looked down on in the neighborhood on the grounds that she was not able to earn as much money as she expected. She thought at the very least that her migration had been a total failure. Furthermore, in utter despair, she was also fearful of facing discrimination and prejudice because of her personal history of pregnancy before marriage and subsequent time in prostitution. Once the gossip of her personal experience was circulated in her home village, the neighbors would surely say that she was a disgrace to her family, which she also feared.

A Place Rife with Violence and an Unstable Living Environment

Chariya migrated to Poipet primarily for the purpose of supporting her family economically and intended to work temporarily. During the time she was working there, one part of Poipet was hardly safe and was rife with drug trafficking and smuggling, gang fights, thefts, and sexual violence.

Comments about the situation in Village A and Village B were "the outer wall made of cardboard was cut with a knife"; "sandals and clothes put outside were stolen"; "a violent and noisy fight always broke out, and a week ago there was a fight of gangs"; "the sight of violence where a wife was beaten by her husband was seen regularly"; and "there was always someone shouting angrily."

In a place in which migrants live, neighboring residents rarely share their personal information and backgrounds with each other, and they tend to keep each other at a distance. In particular, in an area where peace is unstable, residents are more likely to show indifference to the concern of others. This is probably supported by the remarks collected from the interviews with residents. For example, a resident says that "as the mobility of people was intense, people did not know each other well. In the village where I used to live, the village leader took the leadership and village members worked together. In the place where I live now, it is unlikely to happen. It is hard to trust anyone."

In general, violence is likely to run rife in the place where it is comparatively difficult for mutual support to function smoothly as safety net. The situation as such is likely to cause not only direct violence but also structural violence. The former is defined as a brutal act intending to hurt or damage someone physically or mentally, and its performer is visible and can be specified. As to the latter, unlike direct violence, its performer is invisible and cannot be specified. *Structural violence* is the term used to describe the situation where the social structure in itself exerts such negative influences as poverty and inequality.

Within this structure, Chariya was a single woman migrant, suffering from economic poverty, and she had no one to count on. She was in a social environment in which these negative conditions all worked to her serious disadvantage.

Conditions of Going Back to One's Home Village

In the rural villages of Cambodia, premarital sex tends to be considered as a deviation from the gender code of women, even if it results from sexual violence. This is applied to the case of Chariya, when her pregnancy was criticized as disgrace on the family. In the end, she was abandoned by her family and had no other path but to leave her village for Poipet, despite the fact that she had nowhere to go particularly, and she was then pregnant. In Poipet, looking for a job, she got to know a broker through the introduction of her friend. Then she was trafficked and sold by the broker to a brothel when she was four months pregnant.

Afterward, she was taken into protective custody by the police, but she did not go back to her home village. Instead, she returned to Poipet again. Although she actually thought that she wanted to go back home, she had a good reason for not doing so. In fact, she was afraid of confronting discrimination and prejudice on the grounds of her personal experience of prostitution. In addition, she was fearful of the gossip that would circulate in the village that her migration was a failure, without earning much money.

Not only Chariya, but also other women migrants confessed that they actually feared failure in their migration. When interviewed, some of them answered thus: "they could not go home, because they did not live up to their family's expectations yet" and "they could not yet earn as much money as they expected." Considering the actual situation in which migratory workers are, earning their daily bread is all they can do, and sometimes it is difficult for them even to earn money for the day.

Some migratory workers decide to stay longer until they live up to the "conditions" of going back home. At first, they plan to stay and work for a short period of time. However, if they cannot earn so much money as to meet the expectations of their family, they probably extend their term of stay to get "qualification" to go back home in a favorable and desirable way.

Even when a woman migratory worker is victimized by human trafficking and later on she is taken into protection, it is not sufficient for assuring her personal safety. This is probably because in Cambodian society a woman migrant holds herself back from going home once she has been labeled as one whose behavior deviates from the gender code. She also comes under immense pressure as a result. The only choice left for her is to lose herself in the place where job openings are always available and the mobility of people is active. This means that she has to go back to the place where poverty is reproduced and human trafficking is rampant. Therefore, in preventing the recurrence of human trafficking, it is necessary to consider individual social backgrounds and the conditions of those who hesitate to go back to their home villages.

SUMMARY

Human Trafficking in Poipet and Its Victims

In the development of the market economy, rural villages are in the process of dissolution. There are quite a few families who have deepened their poverty because of parting with their land or by running up debts caused by unexpected events such as contracting illness. These people come to Poipet to look for a job, drawing a picture of a better life and economic success in their imagination. However, whether they live in the rural village or in the border area, wherever they are, in fact, it is not a simple matter for the socially vulnerable to turn their lives around for the better.

The mobility of people is one of the features typical of the border area, and this partly contributes to the absence of a regional community, a community rooted in the neighborhood which functions as the system of mutual support among community members in the rural villages of Cambodia. However, without mutual support rendered by a community, migrant workers in the border area have to earn cash income by themselves in the market economy. This is a social environment in which people are connected with each other by commercial and economic value, not by a solidarity shared with neighbors as they would have in the rural village. Living in such a society, and without having awareness, people are turned into commodities and made the targets of trafficking. At present, "trading in humans as commercial items" is conducted not only in Cambodia and Thailand but also in the Greater Mekong, and it further connects with the global market of human trafficking through the transnational network.

NOTES

1. It is not only UNHCR and UNBRO, but also other UN agencies such as the United Nations Children's Fund (UNICEF), the World Food Programme (WFP), and the Food and Agriculture Organization (FAO) of the United Nations, which contributed. (UNTAC Documentations, and Cambodia Peace keeping Documentations, accessed December 27, 2018), https://peacekeeping.un.org/sites/default/files/past/unt acbackgr2.html.

2. The numbers vary greatly depending on the source. Numbers vary from 350,000 persons to 360,000 persons even according to UN materials. According to Cambodia Peace keeping documentations, "UNHCR had determined that there were more than 360,000 potential returnees, of whom over 90 per cent were under the age of 45 and almost half under the age of 15. Some 60 per cent of them originated from the provinces along the Thai-Cambodian border, and over two thirds of them had lived in the refugee camps along the border for over a decade." (https://peacekeeping.un.org/sites/default/files/past/untacbackgr2.html, accessed December 27, 2018).

3. UNTAC Documentations, and refer to Cambodia Peace keeping documentations, by the end of April, 5,763 people had returned. "Concerns were being raised, however, that because of the difficulty of finding suitable mine-free land for the returnees, the congestion of urban areas, the unsatisfactory health situation within the country and the delays expected during the rainy season, a number of the returnees would be unable to take part in the electoral process."

4. Village A and B names have been changed to protect victims' identity.

5. Because this research deals with victims of human trafficking and their families, and victims of sexual violence, following the duty to protect privileged information, the sites of Village A and Village B are kept unidentifiable. Village A was actually given a site number (when researched) but, including this number, anything concerning its site is kept unidentifiable.

6. Interview with the NGO staff in Poipet on August 25, 2006.

7. Interview in Village B on September 10, 2006.

8. When a follow-up survey was conducted in August 2013 concerning work in the area close to the border with Thailand, Cambodian workers went into wage talks and disagreed with the proposal of 120 baht per day because it was much cheaper than they expected. Instead, they worked for the payment in the range of 130 to 200 baht a day. However, the minimum wage paid in Thailand is 300 baht per day. Thus, Cambodian workers only receive the payment which is less than the minimum wage in Thailand.

Chapter 3

The Modern History of Cambodia and the Present Situation of the Rural Village

In Cambodian society, social unfairness and regional disparities remain persistent, and a distorted social structure causes problems such as income gaps and divisions in the quality of life between rural areas and urban areas. The oppression of the poor and needy also presents a distortion of the social structure. In order to get a better understanding of the social and cultural structure creating regional inequality in Cambodia, it is helpful to survey the modern history of Cambodia, especially the history after the liberation from French domination. The modern history of Cambodia can be described as a history of disruption. After independence from France, several foreign nations intervened and interfered in the domestic affairs of Cambodia. As a result, internally Cambodia fell into disruption and instability, and externally came into a deadlock in diplomacy.

In the second half of the 1990s, social distortion grew further and its influence is still felt in the expanding economic division between rural areas and urban areas. This is partly because Cambodia made a sudden shift to be incorporated as a part of the world capitalist economic system before building up the national strength in a proper and steady way. The underlying cause can be explained by the fact that shortly after independence, internal power struggles, one after another, deprived Cambodia of the chance to lay a solid foundation for future economic development. The modern history of Cambodia is so complicated that it becomes very difficult to grasp it both in its entirety and in its details. Nonetheless, this chapter attempts to present an outline pertinent to the gist of the modern history of Cambodia.

INDEPENDENCE AND THE INTERNAL STRUGGLE FOR POWER: THE INTERVENTION AND INTERFERENCE FROM THE INTERNATIONAL SOCIETY

Cambodia gained independence from France under King Sihanouk in 1953. In 1955, Sihanouk abdicated his throne to engage in the political movement. At that time his father assumed the throne while Sihanouk established a political party and eventually became prime minister. Sihanouk formed the People's Socialist Community, *Sangkum Reastr Niyum*, as the political base on which he had come to power. *Sangkum* was a political party and ideologically embraced a mixture of socialism and democracy, based on Buddhism following the religious tradition of Cambodia. Sihanouk's government tried to pursue moderate policies, taking a course between the right wing and the left wing. During the Cold War, Sihanouk tried to maintain neutrality in diplomacy. With support garnered from the Western bloc and the Eastern bloc, Cambodia concentrated on developing the nation's agriculture and industry to consolidate the national infrastructure. The Cambodia of the 1960s comparatively gained political and social stability, and the capital city of Phnom Penh had a popular reputation as "Paris of the East."

Although neutrality was the chief characteristic of Cambodian diplomacy at the time, it was also characterized by competing internal factions trying to maintain a balance and thus came to be understood as "tightrope diplomacy." Unrest in the international situation caused domestic instability: a political dispute over "who would be in power?" developed. The struggle for power was split into three major feuding groups: the pro-American faction, the pro-China faction, and the Communist group. Afterward these three groups were exposed to international political intervention.

In prosecuting the Vietnam War, the United States aimed to cut off the so-called Ho Chi Minh Trail, the route to transport logistic support from North Vietnam to the National Liberation Front (NLF) in South Vietnam. Because of necessities arising from military operations, the United States wanted to secure Cambodia as a place of strategic importance and offered support to Marshal Lon Nol, a Cambodia politician and American sympathizer. Lon Nol, backed by the United States, launched a coup d'etat against Sihanouk who was pro-China and assumed an anti-American attitude. Lon Nol ousted Sihanouk to seize control over Cambodia and established the new nation called "the Khmer Republic." The Lon Nol regime let the United States enter Cambodian territory for the execution of military operations in the Vietnam War.

Following this, aerial bombing campaigns were developed, along with the installation of land mines in rural villages in the vicinity of the national boundary with Vietnam, causing heavy casualties among the Cambodian population. In parallel with these bombing raids, an armed conflict arose between the forces of Lon Nol and those of Sihanouk in alliance with Pol Pot (with the Communist Party of Kampuchea).[1] Cambodia became impoverished by the domestic political dispute coupled with being embroiled in the Vietnam War. The two-front war brought devastation to the infrastructure of the rural villages inside the territory of Cambodia. It brought about extensive damage to the life in the rural villages and exhausted people, causing great disorder.

After the coup carried out by Lon Nol, Sihanouk joined hands with the Communist Party of Kampuchea, also known as the Khmer Rouge,[2] forming the Royal Government of National Union of Cambodia (RGNUC) in order to resist the pro-America Lon Nol government.[3] On the 17th of April in 1975, five years after hostilities opened against Lon Nol, RGNUC won a victory in the Civil War. Afterward, the Khmer Rouge Army led by Pol Pot entered into Phnom Penh and brought the capital under control. Pol Pot declared the establishment of the State of Democratic Kampuchea (the Pol Pot regime from 1975 to 1979).

The Pol Pot government attempted to realize a society based on communism and collective farming, nullifying capitalism, the traditional family system, Buddhism, worship of king, and Western thoughts. The communist regime also abolished social systems such as currency, market, family registration, and education. Architecture in urban areas was also destroyed. Only forced marriage was authorized by the communist government. The Khmer Rouge disintegrated traditional family relationships and the mutual support system particular to the Cambodian rural community, ensuing from the negation of the conventional marriage system. The entire population of Cambodia was forcibly sent into farming areas in the provinces and resettled in People's Communes, called "*Sahakoh*." Whether adults or children, the people were forced into compulsory labor and engagement in farm work. Authorities confiscated all personal property and placed it under state control. Pol Pot attempted to clear away the old Cambodia and create a thoroughly new society as he had conceived, pushing forward radical and extreme communization.

During this reign of violence lasting three years and eight months, estimates of the number of victims range from 1.7 million to 3 million. The Khmer Rouge suppressed and massacred supporters of the former regime, wealthy people, intellectuals and students, and religionists by violence, torture, and execution. An enormous number of citizens died from starvation, malnutrition, and illness caused by poor health conditions and lack of medical care. Schools and Buddhist temples, formerly places of great spiritual support, were turned into slaughter sites.

The Pol Pot government set forth anti-Vietnam sentiment and took sides with China, whereas Vietnam took a pro-Soviet line. The relationship between Cambodia and Vietnam was seriously impaired, and a border dispute between the two nations broke out. Eventually it developed into a fierce battle. In December 1978, Vietnam launched an invasion into the territory of Cambodia. On the 7th of January, 1979, Heng Samrin with support from Vietnam gained control of the capital city of Phnom Penh and ousted Pol Pot from power. Pol Pot fled with the Khmer Rouge Army to the border area close to Thailand. Vietnam established the People's Republic of Kampuchea (PRK) and stood behind Heng Samrin. The pro-Vietnam Heng Samrin regime kept Vietnamese forces stationed in the territory of Cambodia. The international community, apart from several nations such as the Soviet Union, Eastern Europe, and India, did not acknowledge Cambodia as a sovereign nation but rather a Vietnamese puppet government.

Internally Heng Samrin's government faced resistance from three factions: the Pol Pot faction (the Khmer Rouge), the Sihanouk faction, and the Son Sann faction. The three resistant factions joined hands together and formed the Coalition Government of Democratic Kampuchea (CGDK, the Coalition Government)[4] in 1982. The international community, mainly Western nations, regarded the Coalition Government as the official representative of Cambodia and granted it a seat in the United Nations. The Coalition Government officially signed and joined the United Nations as early as December 1982. The international community formally approved the Coalition Government consisting of the three factions, one of which was the party led by the Khmer Rouge. This indicates that the international community overlooked the wholesale killing and destruction committed by Pol Pot. The affair left an indelible stain on the reputation of the international community.

Despite the fact that the Coalition Government established a new government six months before gaining membership in the United Nations in 1982, the newly built government lacked unity in national governmental organs and operated without proper governing functions. Each of the three factions arbitrarily decided the politics and military policies in its own way. In appearance there was an administrative body but in substance it hardly functioned as "government." Anti-Vietnam sentiment was the single point in common to the three parties.

The internal situation was further complicated by the fact that the global community had extended legitimacy to the Coalition Government. In Cambodia two governments at odds existed at the same time: the PRK led by Heng Samrin and the CGDK. The former functioned practically to govern a large part of the nation, acknowledged not by the international society but by socialist nations such as the Soviet Union (Russian Federation). The latter lacked administrative functions but received an official guarantee from the international community. Even after the collapse of the Pol Pot regime (the Khmer Rouge), Cambodia continued to pursue a full-scale Civil War over power for more than a decade. There were foreign nations behind each faction. The intervention of foreign nations complicated the situation more seriously. As a result, it took Cambodia a long time to terminate the internal struggle for power.

After the end of the Cold War, the international community began to make a concerted effort to build peace in Cambodia. In seeking peace efforts, international meetings were held at home and abroad,[5] one of which was the First Jakarta Informal Meeting. This was a conference which took place unofficially to grasp the actual state of the Cambodian Civil War. In the meeting the leaders of all the factions and the parties concerned met together for the first time: the Heng Samrin government, the Sihanouk faction, the Pol Pot faction, and the Son Sann faction were joined by Vietnam and the Association of Southeast Asian Nations (ASEAN).

The meeting was convened to bring about peace between the governments at odds, but to no avail. Afterwards, Heng Samrin made a sudden announcement about the establishment of his independent government in April in the year of 1989 and changed the name of the country from the People's Republic of Kampuchea to the State of Cambodia. Meanwhile the Coalition Government responded to the announcement with stiff resistance and launched an all-out attack on the Heng Samrin Army. As a consequence, the armed conflict between the two parties went from bad to worse. Moreover, guerrilla warfare by the Pol Pot Army intensified in strength. During the period from 1989 to 1991, the Civil War raged without any favorable sign of termination.

Following the breakdown of the Cold War structure, the international society entrusted peace efforts toward Cambodia with the United Nations. The United Nations took the leadership in seeking a political solution to the situation in Cambodia and launched UNTAC. When *Agreements on a Comprehensive Political Settlement of the Cambodia Conflict*[6] (the Paris Peace Agreements) were concluded in 1991, UNTAC was granted the complete authority to exercise supervision of Cambodia. In March of the following year, 1992, UNTAC was inaugurated. For eighteen months until September 1993 the United Nations Peacekeepers were stationed in Cambodia under the direction of UNTAC.

The duties UNTAC were assigned were forming an election organization and conducting a fair election; provisionally managing and assuming administrative responsibility for diplomacy, defense, national finance, public peace, and information for the period from the time after the first election till the formation of a new government; supervising and inspecting the evacuation of foreign armies; promoting protection of human rights; helping the resettlement of refugees and displaced persons; and reconstructing and reviving the nation. In May of 1993, the first general election was called. A newly established government organized a coalition cabinet with two prime ministers elected: Prince Norodom Ranariddh as first prime minister[7] and Hun Sen[8] as second prime minister. In September of the same year, the new constitution was promulgated, and Sihanouk came to throne again as the King of Cambodia. In 1998 when the second general election took place, the Cambodian People's Party carried out another election. As of 2020, the Hun Sen regime has been in power for over two decades.

ECONOMIC GROWTH AND THE REALITY

Market Economy and Cambodia— Who Is the Development for?

While UNTAC was stationed in Cambodia for eighteen months, an enormous amount of foreign money, called "UNTAC Money," flowed into the market of Cambodia. According to the data released by the United Nations, Cambodia accepted two billion dollars in investment and 26,000 foreign residents.[9] It can be safely said that after the Civil War came to an end, a large amount of foreign aid from governments and international organizations and foreign money from foreign residents opened the way for Cambodia to shift to a market economy. The constitution promulgated in September 1993 already specified the promotion of a market economy in the nation. Following the withdrawal of UNTAC, Cambodia still depended substantially on foreign aid but set out to introduce a market economy into its economic system. In parallel to working on economic development, Cambodia set forward internationalization, joining ASEAN in 1999 and the World Trade Organization (WTO) in 2004.

For the decade from 1993 to 2003, the growth rate of Gross Domestic Product (GDP) in Cambodia increased by 6.3 percent on average. By looking at the ratio of real GDP by industry, agriculture marked the highest rate, ranging between 30 percent and 40 percent in real terms. However, in the 2000s manufacturing industries produced remarkable growth in the ratio of GDP: in 1993 marking 8.9 percent growth, while in 2003 increasing to 19.6 percent. With reference to the breakdown by types of industry, among the manufacturing sector, the garment industry remarkably moved ahead in growth and formed a significant percentage of the GDP ratio, increasing from 12 percent in 1993 to 70.8 percent in 2005.[10] The enforcement of the Foreign Investment Law provides some background to the conspicuous growth of the garment industry as one of the leading industries in Cambodia. The law enabled foreign affiliated companies to find entry into the garment industry more freely. From 1996 onward, an increase in the growth rate was backed up by the fact that the United States granted Cambodia the Most Favored Nation status (MFN) in 1996 and Generalized System of Preferences (GPS) in 1997. After Cambodia obtained the position of MFN, Taiwan, Hong Kong, and nations of ASEAN such as Singapore entered into the garment industry in Cambodia for the purpose of exporting products to the United States. In short order, large factories were built intensively in the capital city of Phnom Penh and the surrounding districts. At present, the Garment Manufacturers Association enrolls 589 garment and footwear companies. The business has hugely expanded into a significant industry to employ over 630,000 workers in all.[11]

Generally, foreign affiliated companies look for a place wherever labor costs and land values are as low as possible. Following the trend of the world market, multinational companies seek to take advantage of capital investment. From the viewpoint of profitability, many multinational companies have been able to shift production to Cambodia because Cambodia meets necessary and sufficient conditions, offering lower labor costs and land values. As the capitalist economy gradually overtook the economic system in Cambodia, the significance of the world market has increased for the garment industry, which has expanded into a leading business to earn profits and support the national economy. In the globalized economy, multinational companies try to find cheap labor costs wherever available, making Cambodia a location fit for globalization.

After 2004, Cambodia steadily continued its economic expansion. During the period from 2004 to 2007, the growth rate in GDP topped 11 percent on average. Between the years of 2008 and 2009, Cambodia's economy stagnated due to the economic depression in the US money market caused by the "Lehman Shock." At one time Cambodia marked 0.1 percent in the GDP growth rate. Before the recession, exports from the Cambodian garment industry to the United States accounted for 66 percent of total exports. A sharp fall in exports at this time indicates that Cambodia came under significant influence of the economic recession caused by the collapse of the major banks in the United States. The Cambodian economy depended heavily on the garment industry, which in turn relied on foreign capital. In the sense that the flow of foreign capital directly affects Cambodian national growth, the worldwide economic crash extending over Cambodia brought out the vulnerability in its economic autonomy. In 2010 the year after the economic downturn, the Cambodian economy turned the corner to pick up, marking a figure close to 6.0 percent in growth rate.

Every year following 2010, the Cambodian economy continued to show growth of around 7.0 percent. The steady economic growth can be attributed to an increase in the exports of the garment industry and other manufacturing industries; the development of tourism; expansion of the construction industry chiefly in the capital city of Phnom Penh; and engagement with foreign affiliates and foreign investment as part of national policies. In recent years, the increase in exports from the garment industry has been one of the key industries supporting the national economy. The industry has expanded its market from primarily the United States to encompass a range of EU countries.

From 2005, Cambodia went through a major transition to further economic growth. In order to realize its goals, the government of Cambodia set up Special Economic Zones (SEZs) as part of the national policies concerning urban development, and engaged in the introduction of foreign capital. SEZs are a system which provides foreign affiliated companies with legal and administrative privilege to locate production facilities and build factories in the areas designated as SEZs. At the moment, there are eight regions selected as SEZs: Koh Kong, Phnom Penh, Svay Rieng, Sihanoukville, Poipet, and others. In these SEZs, 228 foreign affiliated companies are registered (as of 2018). In 2014 there were twenty-four places designated as SEZs but by March 2015 this had increased to thirty-four places. The introduction of direct investment from foreign countries contributed to this expansion. For example, the government encouraged Chinese companies to locate production in the SEZs (the plan known as China plus One) and also worked on a similar "Thailand plus One" and "Vietnam plus One," setup for the purpose of the division of labor between the countries in the Mekong River basin.

The SEZs and the garment industry both contribute to Cambodia's economic growth, and both players display profitable activity nationwide. SEZs are not limited to urban areas but are also found in several provinces. The same is true of the garment industry: factories are present in the suburbs and provinces as well. Notably in Cambodia GDP per person is increasing and almost every sector is growing yearly.

However, in actuality, it is a few large cities that have the full benefit from economic development. Vested interest groups of privileged members living in large cities gain benefits and profits generated by an increase in GDP. Meanwhile, farmers in rural villages receive much less benefit brought by this economic growth. Agriculture is still one of the key industries for the people of Cambodia. Nonetheless, it is actually quite difficult for most farmers to depend on full-time farming as their main source of livelihood. In order to gain more cash income, many people migrate from the rural villages. Nowadays, migrant labor is a practice commonly adopted in rural villages.

Economic development widens the income gap between rural areas and urban areas. Although at a national level the economy of Cambodia grows in most sectors, the specific sectors essential to improve national life fail to show much growth. While limited sectors show remarkable economic development, disproportionately raising the overall growth rate, not all market sectors show equally high growth. In fact, economic progress is creating a growth in the income gap not only between rural areas and urban areas, but also among city dwellers. This is the point necessary to make close observation.

The Gap between the Urban Area and the Rural Area

In Cambodia, the poverty line is defined by the National Institute of Statistics (NIS), which conducts the Cambodia Socioeconomic Survey and collects the data to calculate the poverty index, conceptually with reference to income poverty as the basic guideline. During the period between the years 2005 and 2007, when the persons whom I interviewed were trafficked, GDP in Cambodia per person was valued at US$485 in 2005 and at US$656 in 2007.[12]

In order to improve the high percentage of poverty nationwide, the government of Cambodia formulated national strategies one after another, starting with the National Programme to Rehabilitate and Develop Cambodia (NPRD). This was followed by the First Five-Year Socioeconomic Development Plan (SEDP I) between 1996 and 2000; the Second Five-Year Socioeconomic Development Plan (SEDP II) between 2001 and 2005; the National Poverty Reduction Strategy between 2003 and 2005; and the National Strategic Development Plan between 2006 and 2010.

The period between the years 2004 and 2010 saw the Cambodian rate of poverty moving down slightly: 34.7 percent in 2004; 30.1 percent in 2007; and 25.0 percent in 2010. In terms of the gradual decrease in numerical figures, poverty endemic to the nation appears to mark a decline. However, looking at the poverty percentage by region, in 2004 rural areas accounted for 39.2 percent, Phnom Penh 4.6 percent, and other urban areas except for the capital city 24.7 percent. However, in 2007, the poverty rate in rural areas was 34.7 percent, Phnom Penh 0.8 percent and other urban areas 21.9 percent. The poverty percentage of Phnom Penh dramatically dropped, whereas the other two groups remained almost at the same level. The figures show that there was still a wide gap in income between the capital city of Phnom Penh and other regions. Even though the government of Cambodia has taken strategic measures for poverty reduction, improvement has not yet been uniform on a national scale.[13]

Rural villages of Cambodia have a dense concentration of poverty. At all times, the government of Cambodia has addressed the reduction of poverty as high on the national agenda. A high percentage of poverty endemic to rural villages emerges as a social problem in correlation with low-income farming. According to the statistics provided by the World Bank, the farming population of Cambodia amounted to 71 percent in the year 2006, and out of this percentage, the poor accounted for 91 percent. This indicates that those who were engaged in farming in rural villages lived a life under the poverty line. Unless there is a break in the situation in which low productivity of farming leads to low income, the poverty in rural villages remains persistent. It can be pointed out that as the farming population in the rural village grows, population living in poverty also grows in number.

In considering poverty in rural Cambodian villages, the low productivity of farming is likely to hamper the reduction of poverty. In rural villages there has been little change in the method of farming since the 1960s. In many villages, the traditional farming method is popularly adopted: plowing by cow/ox and employing draft cattle; cultivating crops along the river by utilizing natural land features; and harnessing rainwater. A feature of traditional farming methods is that they are manual labor-intensive.

Today, advertisements for farming tractors are placed here and there in the rural villages. Advertising farm machinery and implements to enhance productivity can be effective to some extent, but it has actually produced only a partial change. The spread of farm mechanization and the introduction of modernized farming techniques have not yet been fully attained. Generally speaking, the advancement of farming methods in rural villages of Cambodia is much slower in progress compared with other countries, because of the consequences inflicted by the Civil War.

A slowdown in enhancing farming productivity can be attributed to the state of arable land utilization particular to Cambodia: landmines planted during the Civil War prevent the expansion of arable land. According to Cambodian Mine Action Center (CMAC), millions of landmines are still left in the ground throughout Cambodia, and it takes a considerable time to clear all of them. The number of incidents involving landmines and human victims has decreased in number year after year, and many people now consider it past history. Nonetheless, numerous unexploded shells and landmines continue to pose a danger, especially in the northern region and the interior of farming villages where poverty-stricken farmers live. For the sake of safety, it is still difficult to bring land under cultivation because of a shortage of arable land.

It is generally recognized that the government redistributed land equitably after the termination of the Civil War. However, the data from the National Institute of Statistics in 2004 already exhibited that the percentage of farmers without their own arable plot was on the increase. According to the research,[14] in 1997 the percentage of farmers without an arable plot was 12.6 percent, and in 2004 it increased to 19.6 percent. The increase in percentage is closely related to poverty regularly found in the rural farming village. Particularly, farmers in tight economic situations have parted with their arable plots. In general, they submit themselves to a lower position in the hierarchy of the village community partly because they are poor and needy. Owing to their economically weak situation and marginalized position in the power relationship in the village, less favorable and smaller plots are portioned out to them. With poor productivity, it is difficult for them to depend financially on full-time farming. In the end, their household economy comes to a standstill for want of cash income. To make up the shortage of income, they have to sell their property as a final resort for gaining cash. Farmers who have parted with their property leave their home villages and migrate to large cities in order to earn a livelihood.

By taking a look at the population by region surveyed for the decade from 2004 to 2014, urban population shows a slight increase in percentage. The increase can be explained as the growth of migration by farmers from rural areas. Nonetheless, the rural population remains high in percentage. The vital statistics for the decade from 2004 to 2014 suggest that the population in poverty is still concentrated in the rural farming village. Poverty in the rural farming village means not only the shortage of income but also a life of poor quality due to an incomplete infrastructure. In the sense that improvements in infrastructure can determine the quality of life to some extent, life in the rural village without basic systems and services involves sacrifice of comfort, safety, and health.

The NIS data[15] from the year 2014 clearly indicates a wide difference between urban areas and rural areas in terms of efficient infrastructure. Using the availability of electric power as an example, 99.3 percent of Phnom Penh and 91.7 percent of other cities had electric power. Meanwhile, only 47.3 percent of rural areas had electricity with over 50 percent with no public supply of electric power.[16] Instead, lighting in these rural areas depended on batteries (38.8%); kerosene lamps (9.1%); solar (2.1%); and candles (0.5%).[17]

Access to safe drinking water is another area where it is also possible to detect an appreciable difference between urban areas and rural areas. In general terms, safe water can be defined as "tap water" which is available under the conditions where public water service has been set up. Comparing the percentages of households connected to public water mains in Phnom Penh and rural areas,[18] Phnom Penh scores over 90 percent (90.4% in the rainy season and the 90.5% in the dry season), whereas only 9 percent of households in rural areas are connected (8.6% during the rainy season 8.6% and 9.0% during the dry season).[19] In rural areas, other ways to have access to safe water are to get water directly by drilling a hole in a water pipe and to draw water from a well of which the water quality is controlled. In total, 40 to 50 percent of rural areas have some form of access to safe water while about half of the rural population has no access to safe water (57.2% during the rainy season and 48.8% during the dry season).[20] The ways in which this half of the population gets water are by storing rainwater to use (33% during the rainy season and 3.3% during the dry season); using natural water from streams, rivers, or ponds (11.5% during the rainy season and 22.8% during the dry season); and drawing water from a well of which water quality is unchecked (8.5% during the rainy season and 11.1% during the dry season).[21]

Sanitary conditions are also quite different between urban areas including the capital Phnom Penh, and rural areas. The majority of the urban populations have toilets plumbed into a sewage system to carry raw sewage off through a sewage pipe. The percentages range between 80 percent and 90 percent; Phnom Penh—98.1 percent and other cities 80.2 percent.[22] About a half of the rural population (53.5%) does not have toilet facilities beyond unimproved toilets.[23]

At present, there is still a glaring difference between urban areas and rural areas in terms of income and infrastructure. The GDP in Cambodia is surely and steadily expanding yearly and its positive outcome is felt in the form of economic development. Chiefly, the capital city of Phnom Penh and other large cities achieve economic development and receive financial and social comfort brought by economic growth.

However, this economic well-being has not been extended to rural villages equally yet. Thus, rural farming villages remain poor in productivity and low in income. As long as rural farming villages fall behind in economic well-being, it is difficult to reduce internal disparities. The structure of disparity is duplicated on different scales of the exact same pattern but reducing in size

A Villager Going Back Home from Farm Work. *Source*: ©Yuko Shimazaki.

as the focus on the areas being examined is narrowed: domestic disparities between cities and rural villages; regional disparities between agricultural regions and industrial regions; disparities between villages in a region; disparities between communities in a village. In order to break down the structure of inequality, it is fundamental to reorganize the existing society comprehensively and drastically.

THE CAMBODIAN RURAL VILLAGE
AND THE FLOW OF PEOPLE

Nowadays many people living in rural villages leave their home villages and move to different places seeking employment. Those who migrate to another place, particularly to a large city, find it difficult to make a livelihood in the rural village because of poor productivity in farming. The interviewees for this research originally came from rural farming villages. In order to get a better understanding of the economic situation with which they were faced, levels of consumption spending can serve as a reference. Data for consumption spending for the recent decade, in the research period 2006, shows that consumption of the wealthy increased 45 percent, while the consumption of the needy increased a mere 8 percent.[24] Cambodia's Gini coefficient in 2006 was 0.4, indicating a higher level of inequality in income distribution, compared with other nations in Asia.[25] Cambodia exhibits a wider gap between the wealthy and the needy.

The problem is not just the wide economic gap between urban and rural areas, but also the gap in income within the rural farming villages themselves. Referencing the Gini coefficients per person, for example, Phnom Penh shows a decrease from 0.39 to 0.37, whereas rural villages show an increase from 0.27 to 0.37.[26] From the numerical increase, it can be inferred that economic inequality has already taken hold in the rural villages.

The poverty gap in rural farming villages drives people to migrate. There is a high likelihood that poorer people will leave their home villages in search of work. In order to find work, more migratory workers move to places far and wide, not only within their country but also overseas. For example, migratory workers go to the capital city of Phnom Penh or to neighboring Thailand or overseas, much farther than just the neighboring countries. Serious rural poverty is one of the factors which causes an acceleration in migration. There is evidence to show that the migration of the rural population creates a constant flow of people into the urban population. According to annual growth rates of urban populations, the world average values indicate a range between 2 percent and 3 percent. Meanwhile, Cambodia presents a sharp rise at 5.9 percent in 2005.[27] During the first half of the 1990s, people living in the provinces as a result of the evacuations during the Civil War returned to the cities. From the second half of the 1990s through the 2000s, migratory workers from rural areas expanded the urban population.

There are families living in rural villages whose lives have returned to financial stability as a result of gaining cash income through successful migration to urban areas, or to Thailand.[28] On the other hand, in spite of the goal of migrating to improve their lives, there are families who unexpectedly fall into a negative circle of poverty. For instance, in order to raise funds to move, some families have to sell their small farming plot, becoming property-less, and perhaps losing a place to live in the end. Others have to borrow money without specific prospect for repayment and with the amount due continuing to mount. On top of that, unforeseen contingencies can bring about tragic outcomes not only to the person who set out for migration but also to the family members who are left in the home village. Some are involved in human trafficking, and others come back home having been taken ill. In any case, migration is carried out as the last hope for gaining cash income. Sometimes it offers a way upward from poverty to economic improvement. However, at other times it is true that it incurs a way downward into the negative spiral of poverty.

THE CULTURAL STRUCTURE OF CAMBODIA

The Gender Code

In Cambodia there are gender codes: "*Chbab Pros*" for men and "*Chbab Srey*" for women. The gender code is a set of moral standards for behavior, which men and women are expected to follow strictly.[29] This is accepted by the Cambodian society and exerts deep influence on the consciousness of Cambodian men and women. "*Chbab Pros*," the gender code for men, teaches that men are expected to be strong in body and mind and ambitious. At home, a man should be treated with respect and assume the position of head of a family, being admired as such. However, if a man transgresses the male gender code, he is rarely excluded from society. In many cases, men can escape from severe criticism and discrimination. On the other hand, once a woman does something that contravenes the female gender code, harsh criticism is leveled at her. Specifically, in the rural village where upholding tradition is important, a woman who violates the code is looked upon coldly and her "value as a woman," or femininity, is questioned. In Cambodia, generally speaking, a strict code of behavior is imposed on women, and they are expected to observe it more scrupulously than men. Some change is detectable in the consciousness of women living in urban areas, but the conventional moral consciousness still generally prevails in the minds of people living in the rural villages. This section attempts to examine in what way "*Chbab Srey*," the gender code for women, exerts a deep influence on women victims of human trafficking.

"*Chbab Srey*" the image of "the good woman" has variations such as "the good daughter" and "the good mother." It is handed down from mother to daughter from generation to generation. The gender code forbids premarital sexual intercourse and requires women to take care of the family, to do housework in general, to obey parents, and to follow their spouses as married women. The gender code for women is so strict and detailed that it has a strong influence on fostering and consolidating the moral and social consciousness not only of women but also of men. In the name of the gender code, violence against women is often justified and tolerated in the context of a patriarchal society where men are granted authority over women by the male gender code. Therefore, violence against women rarely emerges as a problem, such as the violation of women's human rights.

Another harmful effect of the strictness of the gender code is that it causes self-reproach, especially in women who have been victimized by violence or abuse. They are highly likely to suffer from guilt, blaming themselves for what has happened to them and feeling ashamed of it. In many cases, victimized women are unwilling to speak about the violence or abuse inflicted on them. Even though they have problems with their spouses and suffer serious physical and emotional damage, they tend to think that this pain is their burden. This is partly because victimized women think that they have somehow broken the gender code and take themselves as disgraced by violence or abuse. Among Cambodian women, there is an apprehension that they might transgress the clear line between the good woman and the disgraced woman as drawn by the gender code.

A proverb well known to people in Cambodia says, "Man is gold and woman is cloth." It means that "Gold has a shine and value. Its brilliance lasts forever. On the other hand, cloth cannot be the same once it becomes torn and stained. Then it is worthless and useless." In other words, once a woman's virginity and chastity are blemished, the value of femininity is diminished. Since virginity in women is regarded in high importance, losing one's virginity before marriage, whatever the reason, exposes not only the woman herself but also her entire family to adverse criticism, and they are labeled as morally degraded. Especially in rural villages where traditional human relationships have been established, a woman can be excluded from a community circle consisting of "good members" who are considered to be right and fair in terms of morality if she has lost her virginity before marriage. If the cause happens to be victimization through human trafficking or sexual violence, a woman is highly likely to blame herself for the incident and feel guilty about it. The misfortune leaves her utterly dejected, and deep despair takes firmly hold of her. Primarily if she is a victim of sexual violence, she deserves to be cared for and put under protection. However, the female gender code labels her a deviator and forces her into exclusion from society.

Educational Situation

The Cambodian educational system adopts "the 6-3-3 system": elementary school education for six years, lower-secondary school for three years, and high school for three years. The constitution of Cambodia stipulates that elementary and lower secondary school education is compulsory for children for nine consecutive years. In fact, there are innumerable problems to be dealt with. For example, there are regional educational differences between urban areas and rural areas. The high percentage of withdrawal of needy children from school also is a problem to solve. Although attendance at lower secondary school has seen positive signs of improvement, access to this level of attendance is not yet uniform.

Elementary school education has seen a steady percentage increase, encouraged by the UN Millennium Development Goals (MDGs).[30] However, one of the major problems is the lower percentage of school children who go on to a further stage of education: many children leave school and do not finish the full duration of compulsory education.[31]

According to Cambodia Socioeconomic Survey (CSES), there is a clear difference between boys and girls ranging from six to seventeen in age concerning the reasons why they leave school.[32] The boys answering, "I did not want to go to school" accounted for 21.9 percent, while for girls it was 15.9 percent.[33] Girls answering, "I must support my family economically" made up 33.9 percent as the top response, whereas for boys it was 24.5 percent.[34] "I have to do housework and chores," was an answer given by 8.1 percent of girls , and 4.8 percent of boys.[35] These differences in percentages show that gender differences determine gender roles.

Parents or adult family members taking care of children show a tendency to regard the education of girls as secondary in importance, because girls are highly expected to do housework or engage themselves in migratory work to earn a part of a family's livelihood. The importance of higher education for girls has been stressed by international organizations and NGOs, but the gender code fixes the roles of girls and women so firmly and exerts such a strong influence on Cambodian culture and society that it surely takes a long time to change the social and cultural consciousness of Cambodia. Still, it is necessary to await the spread of girls' education over the long term.

For the recent decade, broadly speaking, Cambodian elementary school education has improved and rapidly achieved higher standards. However, not all the problems have been solved. For instance, quite a large number of children from economically needy families give up elementary education before completion. The majority of these economically underprivileged children have to leave school because of family migration, involvement in child labor, or engagement in housework. Taking the situation into consideration, it cannot be said that educational opportunities are fully guaranteed to all children of school age, whether boys or girls.

At least elementary school attendance appears to mark a steady increase. Still, a careful examination of the actual state of affairs shows the same social structure as in the past. Children who face difficulties are placed in a position at the lowest level of the hierarchy within the existing social structure. Thus, they are offered the least share of the distribution of educational benefit. As long as the social structure remains the same as found today, girls will continue to be deprived of educational opportunities. This is a reality with which the majority of girls are likely to be confronted.

Such uneven distribution of educational opportunities is a problem attributable to the gender code. The underlying cause of the problem is the consciousness found in a specific social group existing in the old system or in the old organization, which upholds the gender code even though it runs counter to the trends of the times. The gender code is a moral inheritance handed down from mother to daughter for generations and long held to this day. In this way, it has been maintained as a tradition worth preserving. Above all, the gender code permeates the society and culture of Cambodia and helps to mold the social and cultural consciousness as seen in Cambodia today. To a large degree, it determines attitudes and the way of thinking characteristic of the Cambodian culture. In this sense, behaviors and ideas expressed in the social life can be explained as the embodiment of the gender code. In other words, the gender code is the epitome of the cultural and social consciousness of Cambodia in terms of gender rule. Unless the consciousness in which the gender code is deeply rooted is changed, the same problems derived from the old gender code will be reproduced. However, the reverse is also true: if the consciousness is changed, a new gender code to reduce the gender gap and respect gender equality can be created.

The Network of Mutual Support in the Rural Village and Social Exclusion

It is a generally accepted view that no presence of long-lasting organizations or networks voluntarily formed by village members exists in the rural village society of Cambodia. There are several reasons to back up this view. First, without communal property, for instance, a building used as a community center or land used as public open space to be taken care of by community members, there was little chance to strengthen a sense of solidarity in working together for the village community. Second, the Pol Pot regime dissolved the traditional community built on the basis of blood relationships unifying families and relatives into one unit in the village society. Finally, as part of the negative effects of the prolonged Civil War, neighbors were pulled apart and human relationships rooted in the neighborhood were broken. As a result, mutual distrust was felt among people.

However, in actuality, rural villages of Cambodia today certainly build networks of mutual support in which a sense of belonging is developed and shared among the village members, families, and relatives. A sense of belonging is found in many scenes of the everyday life of the rural village: formal ceremonial occasions; Buddhist ceremonies; preparations for annual events; farm work such as rice planting and reaping; and house-building. These scenes symbolize the solidarity shared in the village where individual village members gather together spontaneously and work together for a single task with a common purpose. It affords evidence to show the presence of a mutual support network, which is voluntarily formed by villagers.

The network of mutual support existing today in rural villages is a group formed by a small number of neighbors who know each other well. In the network, the neighbors develop a sense of belonging and share it with each other. When they form a network of mutual support, Cambodians at first judge their neighbor according to various factors and discriminate carefully between who is right for membership and who is not. As stated by Judy Ledgerwood, while building human relationships, Cambodians determine one's own social position relatively based on a judgment of the other person according to a variety of factors such as gender difference, generation, business or political connection, academic background, political status, and others.[36]

Additionally, the Cambodian rural village follows long-standing social and cultural norms. Significantly, these norms serve to distinguish between a person suitable for the neighborhood and a person unsuitable for it and at the same time offer a basis of judgment of the person for building morally and socially proper relationships. A resident who falls short of the norms and is determined to be unsuitable for the neighborhood will probably be excluded from the network of mutual support. The examples cited in the earlier chapters tell of this exclusion, the negative aspect of a closed village society. The victims of human trafficking and people in socially vulnerable positions tend to be viewed as those who violated the social and cultural norms. These people are likely to be made targets of discrimination and excluded from the system of mutual support. The situation in which they are excluded from the community network forces them into isolation and drags them deeper into marginalization. As a result, they end up suffering further aggravation of poverty. Thus, the social structure in the Cambodian rural village can be characterized by two opposite aspects. One is the nature that values mutual support, whereas the other is that which excludes those who do something against the socially and culturally traditional norms.

SUMMARY

Sociocultural Structure: The System Making Cambodian Society What It Is Today

The modern history of Cambodia is a history full of domestic power struggles. There is another part of the history of Cambodia which tells of a nation at the mercy of the diplomatic maneuvering and political tactics of the international community. Rural villages throughout the country were dragged into the two-front war, domestic and external. In rapid succession domestic power struggles exposed the villages to the fires of war, while incessant military operations by foreign armies turned the villages into battlefields.

After the Civil War ended and peace returned, the Cambodian government started to implement strategic measures for the reduction of national poverty, chiefly targeting the rural areas at the top of the national agenda. To this day, a set of national policies mainly aimed at poverty reduction has revolved around the development of the national economy. Although the government has worked on steps to deal with poverty reduction, still there is a wide economic gap between rural areas and urban areas.

In the traditional village typical of the Cambodian rural areas, regional community solidarity is surely felt and displayed in the form of a neighborhood support network. In contrast to the spirit of mutual help fully demonstrated to specific members belonging to the network, the closed rural society often exhibits the tendency to expel and exclude anyone who runs counter to the social and cultural norms from the mutual support network. The social structure of the rural village is incorporated into a rigid hierarchy, the foundation of which is consolidated by the social and cultural norms.

NOTES

1. The Communist Party of Kampuchea (CPK) known as the Khmer Rouge led by Pol Pot.
2. It formed the Royal Government of National Union of Cambodia (RGNUC).
3. "The RGNUC led by Sihanouk as Head of State remained in power until April 1976" (Amer, ed. Peou, 2018, 454).

4. The Coalition Government of Democratic Kampuchea consisted of the Pol Pot faction, the Sihanouk faction, and the Son Sann faction.

5. The international meetings which were held during the period from 1989 to 1992 were the Second Jakarta Informal Meeting; Sihanouk-Hun Sen Meeting in Paris; Paris International Conference on Cambodia; Cambodia Peace conference in Tokyo; and ASEAN Foreign Ministers Meeting.

6. The Paris Peace Agreements were concluded by the four factions: the Heng Samrin regime, the Sihanouk faction, the Pol Pot faction, and the Son Sann faction. Another peace accord was also signed among the four factions. Despite the fact that UNTAC governed and supervised Cambodia, sovereignty was granted to the Supreme National Council of Cambodia (SNC) making up of these four factions. The international community generally recognized that the problem of Indochina came to an end with the conclusion of Paris Peace Agreements.

7. Prince Norodom Ranariddh, leader of the royalist United Front for an Independent, Neutral, Peaceful, and Cooperative Cambodia known as FUNCINPEC, is Sihanouk's son.

8. Hun Sen, leader of Cambodian People's Party (CPP) was named second prime minister.

9. The United Nations S/23613, February 19, 1992, S/23613/Add.1, February 26, 1992.

10. National Accounts of Cambodia 2003–2005.

11. ILO, *Cambodian Garment and Footwear Sector Bulletin*, Issue 4, August 2016 (Phnom Penh: ILO National Coordinator for Cambodia).

12. Currently in Cambodia GDP per capita (current US$) in 2019 was US$1,642 and in 2018 was US$1,512. GDP per capita in 2008 was US$745 and in 2009 was US$745. The GDP rate has risen at a tremendous rate in the last decade. https://data.worldbank.org/indicator/NY.GDP.PCAP.CD?locations=KH (GDP per capita data from World Bank Bata Source, accessed June 5, 2020).

13. According to UNICEF data (2019, electronic edition), there is a wide disparity between rural and urban residents. In rural residences 52 percent do not have access to basic sanitation services whereas 96 percent of urban residences have access (UNICEF, 2019, 248. electronic edition). Moreover, distribution of social protection benefits: top 20 percent of rich people get 46.9 percent of the distributed benefits. However, of people in the bottom 40 percent, only 8.7 percent get social welfare benefits; but of the bottom 20 percent only 0.1 percent have access. It means most of the poor people are not getting the social welfare benefits (UNICEF, 2019, 236).

14. National Institute of Statistics Ministry of Planning (NIS), *Cambodia Socio-Economic Survey* (Phnom Penh: Ministry of Planning, 2004), 7.

15. National Institute of Statistics Ministry of Planning (NIS), *Cambodia Socio-Economic Survey 2014* (Phnom Penh: Ministry of Planning, October 2015, electronic version).

16. Ibid., 20.

17. Ibid.

18. Piped in dwelling or on premises.

19. NIS, 2015, 16. Another data, According to UNICEF data, use of "basic drinking water services" accesses are in urban residences 96 percent, in rural residences 70 percent in 2015. In 2017, urban was 97 percent and rural 73 percent (UNICEF, 2017, 162; UNICEF, 2019, 240). UNICEF statistics does not mention "tap water."

20. NIS, *Cambodia Socio-Economic Survey 2014*, 16.

21. Ibid. This is "Unprotected dug well" (NIS, 2015, 16).

22. Ibid., 19. "Improved toilets" means "improved sanitation facility" that "includes three types which are pour flush/flush connected to sewerage, pour flush/ flush connected to septic tank, and pit latrine with slab" (NIC, 2015, 19).

23. About "54 percent (53.5%) of households in the other rural areas had used unimproved toilet facilities in the dwellings" (NIC, 2015, 19). Unimproved toilets mean "pit latrine without slab/open pit, Latrine overhanging field/water, public toilet (pit latrine/latrine), open land, and other included in not improved" (NIC, 2015, 19). Refer to UNICEF, the percentage of usage of basic sanitation services are: urban 88 percent and rural 39 percent in 2015, and urban 96 percent and rural 48 percent in 2017 (UNICEF, 2017, 162; UNICEF, 2019, 240).

24. World Bank, *Cambodia Halving Poverty by 2015?* (Washington, DC: World Bank, 2006), 26. To make the situation of victims clear, the reference data is for the year of the research period.

25. According to the World Bank, the GINI indices (%) of other countries in Asia were 35.8 percent for Vietnam in 2006, 32.6 percent for Laos in 2002, 33.2 percent for Bangladesh in 2005, 36.8 percent for India in 2004, and 36.1 percent for, Indonesia in 2006.

26. World Bank, *Cambodia Halving Poverty by 2015?* 29, 78.

27. UNICEF, *The State of the World's Children 2006* (New York, NY: United Nations, 2005), 126.

28. GNI per capita (US$) in 2005 compared Cambodia and neighboring countries: Cambodia was US$380, Thailand was 2,750, Lao People's Democratic Republic was 440, Vietnam was 620 (UNICEF, 2006, Basic Indicators).

29. Judy Ledgerwood, *Politics and Gender*, ed. Peou (London and New York, NY: Routledge, 2018), 414–16.

30. According to UNICEF primary school attendance from 2011 to 2016 was 92 percent for males and 94 percent for females. Data for 1996 to 2005 of primary school attendance was 66 percent for males and 65 percent for females (UNICEF, 2006, 18; UNICEF, 2017, 170).

31. From 2011 to 2016 the completion rate to the last primary grade is 41 percent for males and 55 percent for females. Moreover, the ratio of lower secondary school attendance is 47 percent for males and 54 percent for females. Data from 1996 to 2005 for lower secondary school attendance was 17 percent for males and 11 percent for females (UNICEF, 2017, 170; UNICEF, 2006, 18).

32. NIS, *Cambodia Socio-Economic Survey 2014*, 57.

33. Ibid.

34. Ibid.

35. Ibid.

36. Judy Ledgerwood, "Gender Symbolism and Culture Change: Viewing the Virtuous Woman in the Khmer Story 'Mea Yoeng,'" in *Cambodian Culture since 1975: Homeland and Exile*, eds. May M. Ebihara, Carol A. Mortland, and Judy Ledgerwood (Ithaca, NY: Cornell University Press, 1994), 119–28.

Chapter 4

The Victims of Human Trafficking
Analysis, Categorization, and Description

Based on the findings of the survey of the details of trafficked victims, this chapter attempts to analyze the types of people with a high risk of being trafficked. It also attempts to present an entire picture of features typical of the persons victimized by human trafficking. It then makes an attempt to find out why and how they were involved in the victimization of human trafficking in terms of the influences of the existing social structure. By considering the social influence exerted on the victims, this chapter is going to examine the connection between economic poverty, the shortage of income, and relative poverty, which can be intensified when human rights are oppressed. Various factors contribute to the acceleration of the pace of worsening poverty. A common feature of the victims who were interviewed is that they were deprived of opportunities to achieve their well-being in many scenes of life. Furthermore, it was closely related to a negative chain reaction of violence.

In reality, it is extremely difficult to express in numbers the actual victimization of human trafficking because trafficking always produces victims uncounted officially: there are those who cross the national border to enter into a neighboring country and those who are kept in confinement. Fundamentally, it would not be easy at all to grasp the exact number of victims trafficked in the whole of Cambodia. Certainly, much effort is needed to gather statistics on the incidents of human trafficking occurring not only in Cambodia but also all over the world. Nevertheless, the presence of victims provides compelling evidence that human trafficking surely occurs at any time in any place and must be brought to light.

THE AGE AND THE ORIGINAL PROVINCES
OF THE TRAFFICKED VICTIMS

The victim data dealt with in this text was collected during the period from 2004 to 2008, and the age of the interviewees is the age at the time the research was conducted. At that time, organizations within the United Nations and NGOs appropriated funds from a massive budget for measures against human trafficking to be taken in the whole of Cambodia. International organizations, the Cambodian government, and NGOs, domestic and foreign, developed projects on a large scale all across the country. The goals of the projects were as follows: prevention; legal support; protection; rescue; return of trafficked victims to their homes; investigation and prosecution; partnership; and advocacy.

From the interviews taken at that time, the trafficked victims under protection, including those who appeared to be victims, were women and girls between the ages of two[1] and twenty-six. There were twenty-one victims in the age group between fifteen and seventeen, marking the highest number, followed by the age group between eleven and fourteen (sixteen victims). Other age groups and the numbers of victims were: between two and ten, four victims; between eighteen and twenty, two victims; twenty-one to twenty-four, three victims; over age twenty-five, three victims; and one victim of unknown age. A total of thirty-seven persons ranging in age from eleven to seventeen accounted for 70 percent of the whole. In short, the results collected from the interviews indicated that the victimization was concentrated on persons under eighteen years of age, defined as *child* in the Convention of the Rights of the Child. Among the victims, all but one woman was unmarried. The only married woman was sold by her mother-in-law.

As in the past, it was assumed that human trafficking in Cambodia tended to concentrate on women living in the provinces of Prey Veng, Kampong Cham, and Svay Rieng, situated in the southeast of the country, with a high rate of migration to Phnom Penh.[2] However, by taking a survey of the situation overall, it was found that the victimization ranged over almost all the provinces of Cambodia.[3] In particular, the areas close to the national boundaries saw frequent occurrences of human trafficking. For example, the province of Banteay Meanchey produced fourteen victims, and thirteen of these were residents of Poipet. The International Border Check Point with Thailand is in Poipet, and these woman victims were probably trafficked to foreign countries after crossing the border from Cambodia.

As mentioned earlier, there are high incidences of human trafficking in Poipet. The economic, geographical, and historical perspectives of Poipet offer some background to the frequent occurrence of human trafficking. At present, economically it serves as an important transit place in Cambodia for import and export. Since it was designated as one of the special economic zones, it plays a vital role as the foothold of the southern economic corridor within the Greater Mekong Subregion. From a geographical perspective, it has good access to the prosperous Thai market.

From an historical point of view, camps were set up to accommodate refugees and displaced persons during the Cambodian Civil War. After the closure of the camps, a considerable number of people lost their place to live and had no other alternative but to remain in the border area. In coping with the situation, supporting organizations constructed villages in order for them to resettle there. These newly built villages were created artificially for the purpose of accommodating displaced persons, and were dotted around the vacant lots where the refugee camps used to be. The villages along these border areas had the characteristics of a newly risen place. They are different from the typical rural villages of Cambodia where human relations have grown strong roots in the regional community consisting of fixed village members. Unlike the rural villages, in the newer villages there is an unceasing stream of moving people seeking jobs. Poipet attracts migratory workers from rural parts, those who were forced to leave their home villages because of the harm caused by discrimination and prejudice, and people suffering severe poverty. In response to the course of history, the newly constructed villages have accepted migrants who left their original places, looking for a source of living (Cf. chapter 2).

THE ECONOMIC CONDITIONS OF
THE VICTIMIZED FAMILIES

The Types of Jobs and the Working Conditions

According to Cambodia Socio-Economic Survey 2014 from the Ministry of Planning, around 80 percent of the entire population of Cambodia lives in rural areas and is engaged in some form of agriculture.[4] However, the actual state of affairs is that there are only a small number of people who have their own farming plots. Often these arable plots are so small and limited that it makes it difficult for them to depend financially on full-time farming. Looking at the working situation closely, in general the victimized families had no regular job. In most cases, they were engaged in day work, doing a different job from day to day, and sometimes they were out of work.

The economic conditions of victimized families can be categorized as families financially depending on day work and doing different jobs according to either the dry season or the rainy season; those depending on the money sent from other family members who have migrated; those living mainly on borrowed money and repeatedly contracting debts. Finally, in a family headed

Table 4.1   Job Distribution

Type of Job	The Number of Persons
Collecting scrap items, begging	4
Employment agent (broker)	1
Farming day work (including crossing the border)	22
Farming own land	7
Self-employed	2
Fishing	1
Retailing on the street (fruit and vegetables)	9
Without occupation	4
Total	50

Drawn by the author based on the results from the survey.

by a woman, the income source was from gathering and selling wild fruits and vegetables. Day work jobs were farming; selling goods; collecting scrap items; keeping a street stall; and drawing a cart of piled goods (Cf. table 4.1).

According to the interviews taken from the victimized families, a problem common to all of them was that they had been trapped in a negative chain reaction caused by poverty. Life itself was economically insecure, so they were unable to afford the expenses of medical treatment, education for children, and repayment of their debts. When such economic instability lingered, it was highly likely to cause stress and strain in the family. There were several cases where an accumulation of stress led to incidences of child abuse, domestic violence, alcohol dependence, and drug use.

Income and Expenditure

Data about daily income was collected from thirty-nine families out of the total of fifty. Twelve families were in the group with income under 4,000 riel (less than US$1 when researched).[5] Another twelve families were included in the group with income from 4,000 riel to less than 8,000 riel (between US$1 and 2). The figures below US$1.25 (when researched) are below the poverty line. According to the definition of poverty given by the World Bank,[6] many of these victimized families were reduced to extreme poverty. Generally, they were low-income families and had a job in the low-paying industrial sector where, from the outset, the minimum wage was fixed at a lower level. Their only income was from the jobs paying close to the minimum wage. Some families received remittances, but these were irregular in intervals, making it difficult to count on these as the chief source of income. The families without any income source made up 20 percent of all the families researched. The means by which these families made their living were by receiving support from NGOs; begging; borrowing money from their neighbors or money lenders; and selling their property, if they had it, for cash income to make up for the shortage of living expenses.

In its National Poverty Reduction Strategy (NPRS), the Cambodian government fixed the daily numerical figures of the minimum food expenditure and the minimum non-food expenditure per person living in a rural village. The total amounts of both figures were defined as the absolute poverty line applicable to Cambodia.[7] As stated by the government, the absolute poverty line was 1,753 riel in 2004 and 2,367 riel in 2007. All the trafficked victims interviewed had lived with their family members or relatives before being trafficked. Families consisting of four or more people were noteworthy. Considering this household situation, a majority of these families lived below the absolute poverty line as defined by the Cambodian government (see table 4.2).

Data was collected on the expenditures of thirty-one families. Of these, fourteen families spent under 4,000 riel per day and nine families spent somewhere from 4,000 riel to less than 8,000 riel totaling twenty-three families which spent from 4,000 riel to less than 8,000 riel (over US$1 to less than US$2). Expenditures for food were the highest percentage of expenditure with other expenses being drinking water, transportation, medicine,

Table 4.2   Family Income per Day for Those Families Where Income Levels Were Known

Income per Day	The Number of Families
Under 4,000 riel	12
4,000 and over to less than 8,000 riel	12
8,000 and over to less than 16,000 riel	2
16,000 riel and over	4
Irregular	1
No income	8
Total number of families	39

Drawn by the author based on the results from the survey.
Currency unit: riel 4,000 riel = US$1

Table 4.3   Expenditures per Day of the Families Researched for Those Families Where Expenditure Levels Were Known

The Amount of Expenditure	The Number of Families
Under 4,000 riel	14
4,000 and over to less than 8,000 riel	9
8,000 and over to less than 16,000 riel	3
Irregular	5
Total	31

Drawn by the author based on the results from the survey.
Currency unit: riel 4,000 riel = US$1

education, repayment of debt, drinking, and gambling. In table 4.3 "irregular" refers to cases where migratory family members came back home temporarily with some amount of money and the family spent the money then.

In answer to a question about how much money the family had in hand after payment of the expenses listed above, 70 percent of the families answered that "There is no cash left at all." The victimized families, in general, were in extremely tight economic situations, so they could ill afford to cope with unexpected contingencies such as medical expenditures or household crisis. Thus, when someone was taken ill, the family managed to raise the money for the medical costs by borrowing money from others or by selling property if they had it.

Of those asked about the details of income and expenditure, eleven persons were unsure about income and twenty-nine persons were unsure about expenses. There are several reasons for this. First, the interviewees included younger persons unfamiliar with household budgets. Second, in some cases income could not be calculated on a daily basis because it was received so irregularly. Finally, the wages differed according to the jobs they were engaged in. Although they could not cite their earnings and expenses specifically, they gave clear answers to the question about what the living situation was like overall: "We have to borrow money for daily expenses"; "We have meals twice a day, just if we are lucky. Often we had a meal only once a day"; "We have rice porridge only"; "We don't have a proper meal, but water only"; and "We keep alive by picking wild fruit to eat." These remarks demonstrate the severity of their poverty.

With or without Debt; Families without Property

Considering the victimized families from the viewpoint of whether they were in debt or not, it was found that twenty families had debts. Fourteen families were categorized in the group of "families without debt" including families whose data was unknown and families whose credit was too low to permit borrowing, owing to their poverty. As shown in table 4.4, the payment of medical treatment was the top answer about why money was borrowed (seventeen families), followed by brokerage fee and preparation for migration (six) and food and living expenses (four).

Medical treatments for which the families used the borrowed money were diseases caused by chronic malnutrition; inflammation of the intestines and diarrhea because of something which had been eaten or drunk; fever; pneumonia; respiratory diseases such as asthma; skin inflammation caused by unsanitary conditions; injuries from physical violence by a spouse (husband); and infectious diseases such as HIV. Respiratory diseases such as asthma were often found in the families involved in collecting scrap items in "the trash mountain/garbage collection site." In many cases, they developed the symptoms of a constant cough. This was partly because they inhaled gases caused by the spontaneous combustion of substances among garbage.

Usually in Cambodia, people who catch some mild disease or sustain a light injury go to a small private hospital in a village or in a province. Sometimes they make do with medicine they buy at a drug store in the neighborhood. In some cases, folk remedies are adopted for treatment. The victimized families interviewed could scarcely afford to pay for sufficient medical treatment, and they had to cope with the situation only with a minimal amount of medicine. It was noticeable that they had no other course but to leave the disease untreated at a hospital before complete recovery. As a consequence, the conditions became more serious, and finally they were taken to a larger hospital or private clinic in the provincial capital. However, they actually could not afford the treatment. In order to raise the money for medical expenses, they had to sell their property or domestic animals.

Close observation should be paid to the answer "free of debts" which cannot necessarily be interpreted as the literal truth. In fact, this answer included families who had a necessity to borrow but had to refrain, explained as "At the time when we asked to borrow money, we were declined. We were too poor to get credit"; and "We had little chance of paying the money back if we borrowed. So we had no choice but to give up." "Free of debts" does not necessarily mean that the family could easily manage on their cash income. Instead, the hidden meaning was that they were not allowed to borrow money because of their low credit rating, regardless of how much they needed to borrow in order to make ends meet.

Among the families in debt, some had difficulties in paying back the borrowed money as smoothly as they had expected. In one case, the parents urged their young daughter to go to work. In another case, the daughter voluntarily made the decision to go to the border area to look for a job. Additionally, in order to clear up their debts, a family inevitably contrived to raise the money to meet loan payments by selling their property. One more case related to the

Table 4.4   The Purpose of Borrowing

The Purpose of Borrowing	The Number of Cases
Medical expenses	17
Food and living expenses	4
Brokerage fee and preparation for migration	6
Housing	2
Purchase of work tools	2
Total	31

Drawn by the author based on the results from the survey: multiple choices.

loss of property was that a family left the village behind because they were harassed by a loan shark who demanded repayment at exorbitant interest rates and abused them with nasty things and rough language.

Based on the findings from the interviews with fifty families, thirty-one families sold their property for cash to cover medical expenses, living expenses, repayment of loans, and the cost of preparing for migration. The victimized families were in economically tight conditions, so they managed to lead daily life with great difficulty. They always had to cut down on living expenses to the degree where the sustenance of life was close to a crisis. Expenditures for unforeseen contingencies, such as medical expenses, laid a heavy burden on them. To survive the situation, they had to sell their property as their final resort. The sale of the property meant not only the loss of all they had but also, in substance, deprivation of a place to live.

The families surveyed were categorized as a socially vulnerable group, and in addition, they had no property. Families living in the northern parts of Cambodia made up a higher percentage. Earlier studies pointing out that the northern parts showed a larger percentage of families without property confirmed these findings.[8] The reason many families without property lived in the northern areas can be attributed to the social and economic background of the region. After they parted with their property, they had no other course but to leave their home villages for the northern parts, in particular, for the areas near the national boundaries between Cambodia and Thailand. They moved to the border areas where there were job openings for day work available. The border areas show frequent occurrences of human trafficking, likely targeting people under a pressing economic necessity. This being the case, economically vulnerable people, especially after the loss of property, are exposed to a high risk of being trafficked.

A CONSIDERATION OF THE VICTIMIZED FAMILY FROM THE PERSPECTIVE OF RELATIVE POVERTY

The United Nations defines poverty as something that is more than income poverty (economic poverty), giving it a definition from various broad angles. Poverty is interpreted in terms of the deprivation of opportunities in life. The deprivation of opportunities includes the lack of access to social services such as education, medicine, health, and housing, and the denial of cultural rights and opportunities. A life of deprivation is considered a state of relative poverty.

The concept of relative poverty has been adopted in the guidelines to evaluate the achievement of social welfare: Human Development Index of the UN Development Program (UNDP); Gender-Related Development Index (GDI);

Gender Empowerment Measure (GEM); and Human Poverty Index (HPI). The Multi-layered Poverty Index (MPI) employed by the United Nations also deals with the concept of the deprivation of opportunities. It evaluates the seriousness of poverty, taking the levels of access to social services into consideration. In short, the MPI is an index to show the degree of relative poverty. According to the MPI, relative poverty is regarded as more serious than income poverty.

Amartya Sen interprets poverty not just as the shortage of income but also as something that has its rise in a life of deprivation.[9] As stated by Sen, poverty is the state in which people are deprived of the fundamental rights and opportunities in life. "Basic rights" refers to the rights to food, clothing, and housing, as well as cultural and social rights. The advancement of social welfare guarantees the entitlement of the basic rights and the scope of opportunities. Deprivation is also true for the situation in which people live in a poor social environment with a lack of occasions to participate in cultural and social activities. Conditions like this are likely to cause or aggravate poverty, depending on the situation. On the basis of Sen's definition of poverty, this section attempts to examine the circumstances in which victimized families were caught up in trafficking from the viewpoints of relative poverty and the deprivation of basic rights and opportunities.

The Educational Situation of Trafficked Victims

Improvements in education, primarily at the elementary level, have occurred year after year following the "Millennium Development Goals" (MDGs) and "Education for All" (EFA), along with the goals set for the international society to achieve. Elementary school education in Cambodia begins at the age of six with the term of schooling for six years. Research on the school attendance of trafficked victims showed that nearly 60 percent of them had had no chance to receive an education. Every one of those who had been to school gave up their education before they finished school owing to migration, care for their younger siblings, and housework for the family.

Table 4.5 shows the length of time the victims' attended school prior to being trafficked, including both those who left school sometime before victimization and those who left school immediately prior to becoming victims (preschoolers have been excluded). Those who responded "no chance of education," gave reasons such as: "I could not go to school because my family was poor, and still so"; "We could not afford school expenses"; "I worked during the day instead of going to school"; and "I had housework to do for my family."

Even public schools cost the families money: the expenses of textbooks, a set of school uniforms, and probably other expenses. If a family lives far

Table 4.5   The Length of Schooling

Education (including the final school grade)	The Number of Persons
Elementary school education between one year and three years	11
Elementary school education between four years and six years	7
Elementary school education for six years and over	3
No chance of education	28
Total	49

Drawn by the author based on the results from the survey.

away from school, they have to pay transportation expenses. Sometimes teachers request that the children take supplementary classes.[10] Although these extra classes are conducted nominally as supplementary tuition, sometimes they are more than just makeup classes and are close to regular classes in substance. Some school children find it difficult to keep up with their regular classes the next day if they miss the makeup class. Children from needy families find it so often financially difficult to take supplementary classes that a few of them have to leave school.

Generally, the families which were victimized by human trafficking lived on tight family budgets. In most cases, education for their children constituted another financial burden for them. Since they tended to regard their children as important and indispensable workers for the household economy, working opportunities took top priority and education was of secondary importance. Half of the thirteen persons who left school for the purpose of going to work explained that "I gave up education because my mother told me to do so." A victimized woman said that "I wanted to go to school but I could not do anything against my mother's wish" and another woman said that "I could not express my wish to go to school to my mother, absolutely not." These remarks reflect the influence of traditional teachings handed down from mothers to daughters that whatever the mother says and directs the daughter should take it as absolute. This is derived from "*Chbab Srey*," or the gender code for women and girls embraced in Cambodia and passed down for generations. The gender code provides the image of "the good daughter" who should be obedient to her mother and do what she is told to do without question.

Moreover, a negative attitude toward the education of girls prevailed in cases where gender differences determined the priority in education. Economic poverty was highly likely to hinder girls from receiving school education. With limited and tight family budgets, the research showed boys took precedence over girls in attending school. This is confirmed by an interview taken from a victimized woman. Her brothers were allowed to attend school but "not me, because I am a girl. I was told that there was no need for girls to go to school. The thing is that I should go to work, instead."

Multilayered Poverty and Human Trafficking

According to the survey of the household situation and social environment in which the trafficked victims lived, some persons were found to have already been victims of either sexual abuse or of domestic violence, or both, and of other forms of indirect violence, prior to becoming victims of human trafficking. The detailed breakdown of this prior victimization is as follows: victims of domestic violence twenty-seven persons; sexual violence (including attempted rape) twelve. Moreover, there were three persons subjected to discrimination on the grounds of living with HIV-positive family members. In addition, of the total of fifty families, twenty-nine families including the victims themselves had suffered nasty and discriminatory remarks based on their poverty and from the conservative cultural bias peculiar to the rural villages they lived in. In social relations, the victimized families were socially vulnerable and economically underprivileged. Incidents of violence and discrimination were likely to aggravate their poverty, making it more difficult for them to break away from the negative spiral. As a result, they were put in a more serious situation of multilayered poverty.

Domestic Violence

Domestic violence in the context of Cambodia is a general term for family violence including violence against one's spouse and child abuse. This text attempts to define the term as violence against family members in the home. Generally, parents in Cambodia have power over their children, since the social norms grant them the position of authority in the home. None of this research uncovered cases where children practiced violence against their parents. However, because of the power structure in the home, child abuse took place in many of the victimized families: twenty-seven persons were subject to physical and mental violence from their parents. In 60 percent of the cases, the abuser was the mother (birth mother, step mother, and foster mother). Examples of this violence included withholding food; beating with a wood stick or a stone; using abusive language; and child-neglect (failure to nurse and bring up children).

At the same time, another pattern of domestic violence was also recognized in these families, from the viewpoint of a daughter: the father's violence against the mother. This spousal abuse was often behind the mother's violence against the daughter. Generally speaking, there is a tendency of an abused mother to use violence against her children. In the families of the trafficked victims, a negative chain reaction of violence in which an abused person turned into an abuser was formed.

Victimization by Sexual Violence

Before being trafficked, twelve persons of the fifty trafficked victims had already been victimized by sexual assault—rape, attempted rape, and indecent assault. The breakdown of the relationship of the perpetrators to the victims was: the real father (one case); step-father (one); uncle (one); acquaintances in the village (seven); friend in the village (one); and a migratory worker staying in the village then (one) (multiple answers were allowed). Examples of when and where these women were victimized by sexual crimes included while being engaged in farm work; on the way back home; at home during the absence of the parents; and being asked out by the perpetrator who harbored a hidden sexual intention. Furthermore, the victims were forbidden under threat by the perpetrators to talk about what had happened to them. Common to all the cases was premeditation: the perpetrators knew well the patterns of behavior of the targets in advance of committing the offense. According to what the victims explained as the reason they were targeted: "The perpetrator thought I was so poor that I could do nothing about it"; "I was regarded as the last person who would bring an action because he knew I could not afford it at all"; "I was told that the police wouldn't believe what a poor person like me said." To sum up, these remarks indicate that the perpetrators committed the crimes by taking advantage of the weakness and vulnerable position of these women in the village.

In Cambodian rural villages, which attach great importance to the virginity and chastity of women, a raped woman is highly likely to be treated mercilessly in her neighborhood. Her family tends to regard her as a disgrace on the grounds that she has deviated from the gender code accepted in Cambodia.[11] Although she is obviously a victim of sexual violence, the woman most often blames herself for what has happened to her and develops a feeling of guilt. Testimonies from the victims show that when the neighbors came to know about the rape incident, the women were discriminated more intensely and isolated from the community. Even worse, some victims had to leave the village because discrimination against them was so intense that life in the village became unbearable. The victimized women were reluctant to speak of these incidents, afraid of the situation where they would have to face discrimination against them. In many cases they faced threats if they were to speak about what had happened to them. This highlights why rape incidents are rarely brought to light.

Discrimination and Isolation

In rural Cambodian villages, a hierarchy of relationships has been established over time. In general, people are sensitive to other people's backgrounds because one's own position in social relations is determined relative to the background and social position of others. Hierarchical human relationships are formed by such factors as a person's economic conditions, occupation, social status, and academic background (with or without educational opportunities). The trafficked victims whom I interviewed were generally in absolute poverty, engaged in day work under unstable working conditions, and had missed educational opportunities. Of the victims interviewed, twenty-nine answered that they had been "discriminated with nasty remarks about their poverty." The meaning of the words "to be discriminated" can differ according to personal impressions and interpretations. In asking for more precise information as to what they experienced exactly and how they felt, they gave answers such as: "my neighbors avoided and ignored me"; "I was addressed as "filthy" by my neighbors"; "I was reviled as a poor person"; "when they saw me, the neighbors said to me "stink"; and "The neighbors always told me words like "go away." They felt that the neighbors looked down on them and cast aspersions on them with abusive language on a daily basis. Twenty-two of the fifty people interviewed believe that they were discriminated against because of "economic poverty."[12] It showed that the majority of them were the poorest in their home villages.

The interviewees said that "the neighbors would not speak to me. I was avoided and ignored by them" in the village they lived in. Thinking that "they lost touch with the neighbors," the women remarked: "Nobody was around but me alone"; "I had no friend to talk to when I had a problem"; "Nobody would help me"; "I knew the village leader by sight. But I have never talked to him, let alone I would not think of going to see him to talk about my personal problems." Their personal experiences bear evidence of the circumstances in which they suffered exclusion and isolation from the village they lived in.

The exclusion and isolation from a community in the rural village directly connects with the failure of access to the right information that can help to protect oneself against being trafficked. A typical rural village in Cambodia is a closed society with human relationships already fixed. A small circle of mutual help is formed, joined by a small number of neighboring persons, in which information about human relations developing in the village is exchanged and shared between members. Meanwhile, the people like trafficked victims are out of touch with other village members. Correspondingly, they are short of information about human relationships in the village. To put it in an extreme way, had the victims had sufficient information they might have been able to escape being deceived. Being isolated from relations with the small community of mutual help in the village means the loss of safety net, and it ends up increasing the risk of being deceived into being trafficked.

THE VICTIMS OF HUMAN TRAFFICKING AND THEIR BROKERS

The Relationship between Trafficked Victims and Brokers

In Cambodia, there are two ways of planning to migrate: ask an employment agent/broker (*Mehkchoul*)[13] to have a job arranged or, count on "connections" with relatives or acquaintances to ask for a help in getting a job. In the case of migration through the intermediation of a broker, in principle, the broker finds a job and makes all arrangements from the departure of a migratory worker to the arrival at the workplace. An employment agent/broker acts as a go-between whose job is to fill the demand for workers in particular jobs with migrants who are in search of jobs—to bridge the supply of workforce and the demand for workforce. Needless to say, not all brokers are traffickers, and there are always brokers who are trustworthy in making arrangements so that migratory workers can work under better and stable conditions.

Nonetheless, every woman interviewed was deceived into human trafficking by brokers (*Mehkchoul*) at some point during their migration. There are generally two patterns in carrying out human trafficking: a single broker deals personally with every aspect of the trafficking or several brokers are involved in a single case of human trafficking, which is the most common. Various roles in the human trafficking process are distributed respectively to various brokers: looking for target women and girls with commercial value to traffic; undertaking to transport the target to a certain place and assisting with illegal immigration; taking responsibility for crossing the national borders to enter into a neighboring country, whether legally or illegally; and negotiating and discussing business with buyers or employers.

Primarily, persons and families aiming for migration have contact with brokers in order to ask for a job. They then turn to brokers for preparation of everything necessary for their migration, such as securing the means of travelling and the transportation route. At the time of the first contact with brokers, those seeking to migrate already hold the expectation that brokers will be able to bring them economic success. On one hand, as if they were clutching at straws, they entrust all the details of their migration to brokers with the hope that "our living conditions will turn for the better"; and "we wish to get out of the tight living situation like this, if we could." On the other hand, in actuality, brokers appear before targets with a plausible excuse to talk about migration, kindly undertaking the procedures necessary for migratory work. With the chief aim of human trafficking hidden far beneath, they take advantage of the targets' economic and social vulnerability and watch for a chance to trade the targets as commercial items.

An interpretation can be drawn from the relationship between a broker and an economically vulnerable woman intending to migrate as the difference in the ability to control the situation. The broker has supremacy over the target person and leaves pieces of information untold to the target, keeping the situation under control. The woman, on the other hand, tends to fall back on and place her trust in the broker with hope for the future, taking up migration as her final hope for making a livelihood. Over the course of time, a power structure of domination and subordination forms within the relation between the two. It is a power relationship between the total control of a broker in a strong position and the emotional dependence of a target in a vulnerable position.

Relation to Brokers—A Comparison between the Rural Village and the Border Area

Human trafficking intrinsically involves a "broker" who acts as a go-between to fill both the need of a migrant for a job and the demand of the market for workforce. The rural village and the border area have distinct characteristics in this social environment. Accordingly, there are perceptible differences in the way the broker gets in touch with the target victim and in the relationship between the two. In rural villages, generally there are just a few brokers and they are not necessarily permanent residents of the village where the target victims live. Once in a while they appear in the village to look for a commercial item to sell or to acquire information or to find something else relative to their business.

Meanwhile, in the border area a large number of brokers exist, who are as close to one another as neighboring persons living in the same village community. In proportion to the variety of ways of getting a job and the types of job available, whether legal or illegal, various brokers engage themselves in arranging work including working on the other side of the border. Brokers in these areas are not only Cambodians but also Thais, Malaysians, and others from various countries forming networks worldwide.

Brokers in the rural village and the border have different characteristics in the ways of human trafficking. In rural villages, it's usual for the broker to appear occasionally and target a needy family. Once the target is fixed, the broker pays visits to the family often in disguise as a kind and caring person to put them off their guard. Having gained their trust, the broker frequently cites successful examples of migration and urges them to migratory work.

Of those interviewed, only four persons clearly recognized that they asked brokers (*Mehkchoul*) to arrange their migration: the four were aware that they had contact with a professional broker, considering the broker neither as "a friend" nor as "an acquaintance of their family." In the first place, they got in touch with the broker clearly intending to have their job arranged. The rest of the victims, however, regarded the broker with whom they were in contact as someone who seemed more personal to them: "an acquaintance, perhaps a friend of my relative" (eight persons); and "an acquaintance, more like a friend of my acquaintance" (five). In particular, younger victims had a decided tendency to view the broker as "a friend" or "an acquaintance": "someone who helped me to find a job and had all the preparation done for me"; and "someone who had a talk with me about this and that." What they called "a friend" was actually a "broker" or a trafficker in the end. Even after being deceived into trafficking, they still insisted upon recognizing the broker as "an acquaintance of my family" or "a friend socializing on a family basis." One case where a woman was trafficked in the rural village conspicuously shows this tendency. Even when she was undoubtedly sold by the broker, still she denied flatly that the broker was really a trafficker, directing her anger at someone else: "He was the person who expressly visited us many times. How could he sell me off? I believe not him, but someone else must have done so."

In the border area, compared with the rural village, it is much easier for a person interested in migration to find and be in touch with a broker. Unlike in the rural village where the broker personally comes into contact with a target and offers a job proposal, in the border area a person planning to migrate voluntarily makes an approach to a broker. The broker, as an employment agent, then responds with enthusiasm to the request. The broker rarely adopts the disguise of a friend but keeps in touch with the target as a person known by sight in the neighborhood.

Something common to both of these scenarios is the fact that the broker is able to make a fairly good escape from the responsibility of human trafficking. Even though a woman victim realized that it was trafficking and complained about it, the broker would cleverly shift the blame for it onto someone else. This is partly because more than one broker, in fact, many brokers, are involved in the process of a single case. Starting from catching a target to the final stage where the victim is forced into sexual exploitation at a brothel or into compulsory labor, many brokers are involved in roles assigned to them. Making the best of the conditions, they can dodge the responsibility with an excuse saying, "I didn't know that personally." In another example, after trafficking a woman the broker disappeared from the village concerned. When the victim visited him in the place where he used to live, she found that he had already left the village. The absence of the broker certainly prevented the victim from having contact again.

Trafficked women tended to refrain from making further contact with the brokers for fear that they should be sold again. As stated by a woman victim, when she went back to the village where she used to live, she suffered overt discrimination and prejudice because she had been involved in the sex industry. Gossip about her personal history circulated, and there was no end to discriminatory remarks about her, so she had to move to another village. In most cases, the victims were reluctant to go back home in case they should face discrimination and prejudice because they had been trafficked. In order not to attract attention from village members, the victims were more unwilling to come into contact personally with the broker again.

SUMMARY

An Interpretation of Poverty of the Trafficked Victims

Amartya Sen explains that poverty is derived from the socially vulnerable state where the rights and functions to guarantee basic human activities are deprived. When poverty is examined in the context of the social structure of Cambodia, a causal relationship between human trafficking and the socially vulnerable situation can be found, as shown in the figure 4.1.

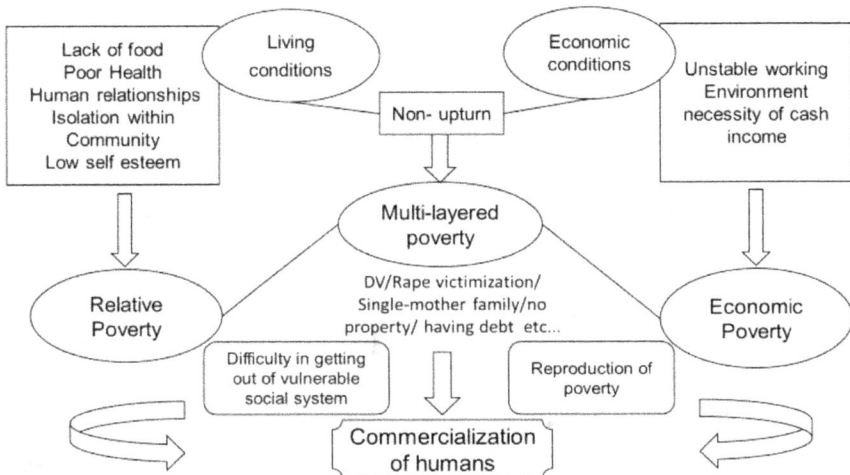

Figure 4.1 The Actual Situation of Victims and Victimized Families due to Human Trafficking.

The victimization of women and girls through human trafficking in Cambodia creates a power structure of domination and subordination within the relationship between the strong and the vulnerable. In other words, those who are in an invulnerable position control those who are vulnerable, and from the opposite point of view, the vulnerable are made subordinate to the strong. As long as power relationships between subordinates and superiors exist in society, vulnerable people continue to arise and are more marginalized by being compelled to subordinate.

Under violence by the name of domination, the rights and opportunities of the vulnerable are oppressed, and this socially vulnerable state is likely to cause poverty. The vulnerable live in an environment where various factors exert a reciprocal influence on each other and create a negative chain reaction of poverty. Human trafficking mercilessly victimizes such needy people who desperately seek to get out of the poverty trap for a better life. As a result, they are sold and swallowed up as commercial items by the human trafficking market following close behind the broker.

The question then arises, "Why and how were the vulnerable women and girls involved in the poverty-generating power structure made up of many different factors?" In order to find answers to this question, a careful survey of their living conditions and social structure is required. The women victims were in utter destitution for lack of cash income to support everyday life. The shortage of cash income, or economic poverty, was caused by the unstable working conditions where they could not necessarily secure a job. Most of them were occupied with domestic worries about how to manage on a small family budget. Under such needy circumstances, they suffered a shortage of nutrition sufficient for the sustenance of life, which in the end affected their health. When they were taken ill, in most cases they found it difficult to cope financially with such an unexpected contingency. In order to cover medical expenses or living expenses, it became necessary to borrow. However, often they had no promising prospect for clearing up their loans. Finally, the amount due kept mounting, and sometimes high interest was added to it. They had no other course but to sell their property for the repayment of the loan. After the sale of the property, they lost the place to live and the plot to farm. As the only means of livelihood, the family without property had to set out for migration to go on for a long period of time.

The majority of these women had neither special skills nor basic literacy skills. Owing to a lack of vocational advantage, most of them were only engaged in low-paying jobs such as day work, cart-drawing, and garbage collecting on the street. Before migration they could not probably conceive that the life as a migratory worker should be so difficult and unstable. For families who moved to the border area, cash was indispensable for buying everything necessary in daily life. Without a cash income, it was certainly difficult to make a living in itself, even to meet the basic needs of food, clothing, and housing. Low-income workers without special skills could scarcely afford to send money to the family left behind in the village. And the family in the village, counting on the money from migration but knowing that there was no money to be received yet, was faced with the necessity of borrowing money for their own living expenses. In this way their amount due was mounting.

In this state of a negative chain reaction of poverty, these vulnerable women not only suffered undernourishment and poor healthcare but also lacked opportunities in life such as access to education, construction of a network of people, and participation in regional society. A state such as this—a life of deprivation—is highly likely to worsen relative poverty. As has been described earlier, there are two perspectives to take up in examining poverty: economic poverty and relative poverty as shown in the figure 4.1. When poverty is aggravated, economic poverty and relative poverty inflict reciprocal influence on each other, where one of these factors can become the cause of the other. Negative effects stemming from the interrelation between the two are, for example, domestic violence, rape victimization, single-mother family, the loss of property, and others as cited in the figure 4.1. Considering the situation of the trafficked women interviewed, discrimination and prejudice were added to these negative factors. The women suffered discrimination and prejudice on the grounds of their personal experiences in the past, just as they were labeled as "disgraced women," following incidents of rape. Afterward, they were isolated and excluded from the neighboring circle, which meant the loss of livelihood to them. They were labeled as a disgrace on the family in the context of Cambodian culture and society, which is determined and molded by the gender code embraced in Cambodia from generation to generation.

The social phenomenon of poverty in Cambodia offers many different aspects and features to be considered. In other words, the vulnerable women lived in conditions of multilayered poverty with various factors affecting each other in a complicated way. By looking at multifaceted poverty closely, it is possible to see the hierarchical relationship between domination and subordination and between the strong and the vulnerable within the social structure of Cambodia. The embodiment of this power structure is perceived on different scales in different scenes of life, such as in neighboring relations in the village community, in family relations, and in gender relations. Having fallen into this social structure, the vulnerable, especially women and girls, are deprived of their human rights, and the situation deteriorates at an increasing rate. At the end of a long and painful process of poverty, human trafficking is ready to seize upon the vulnerable—the ultimate form of the deprivation of human rights.

NOTES

1. Interview with her mother.

2. From author interviews and International Organizations report (ILO/IPEC, 2004). Local NGOs are CCH (Center for Children to Happiness), ECPAT Cambodia, HCC (Healthcare Center for Children), COSECAM (Coalition to Address Sexual Exploitation of Children in Cambodia).

3. The victims of the interviewees come from Prey Veng province (four victims), Svay Reing province (one victim), Koh Kong province (two victims), Kandal province (one victim), Kampot province (three victims), Takeo province (two victims), Banteay Meanchey province (fourteen victims), Battambang province (five victims), Siem Reap province (three victims), Phnom Penh (three victims), Pursat province (five victims), Kampong Thom province (one victim), Kampong Cham province (three victims), and Kampong Chunang province (three victims). (A total fifty victims in the author survey.)

4. According to Cambodia Socio-Economic Survey 2014, measured or estimated population by residence in urban areas, 23.3 percent in 2004, 24.2 percent in 2008, 23.9 percent in 2009 . (NIS, 2015, 3).

5. Then rural areas' villagers calculated 4,000 riel as US$1.

6. The World Bank revised the figure of the international poverty line from US$1.25 to US$1.90 in October 2015. When this research was conducted, the international poverty line (the absolute poverty line) was set at US$1.25.

7. In reference to the definition given in National Poverty Reduction Strategy (NPRS) by the government of Cambodia: the numerical figures are food expenditures calculated to meet the minimum value of the food poverty line (2,100 kilo calories a day) the World Bank (2009, 7, 12).

8. Naoko Amakawa, ed., *Kanbojia no fukko kaihatsu* [Reconstruction and Development in Cambodia] (Chiba: The Institute of Developing Economies, 2001), 285–304.

9. See the introduction.

10. As teachers conduct the makeup classes as a sideline, special fees are to be collected from children. The charge for the makeup classes differs according to the school grade. According to the author's research, the amount ranges from 100 riel to 500 riel, and in a place like Phnom Penh the charge is much higher, for example, 500 riel, 700 riel, and 1000 riel. The fees have increased remarkably year after year.

11. LICADHO, *Violence against Women in Cambodia* (Phnom Penh: LICADHO, 2006), 9.

12. Other reasons for and causes of discrimination are "Living with HIV-positive family members (three cases)," "Rape victimization (two)," "Domestic violence (two)," "Discovery of having worked at a brothel (two)," and "Single-mother family/single-woman (two)."

13. Khmer language (Cambodian language): *Mehkchoul* is an individual who gives information, arranges a job or looks for a job for a migrant worker.

Chapter 5

The Method of Aid and Support in the Border Area

For the last decade, governments, international organizations, and NGOs have worked together in intensifying anti-human trafficking measures, and people have more knowledge and information about human trafficking. As a result, more information about human trafficking has become widely dispersed. On the other hand, this result is accompanied by an ironical effect: human trafficking is more cleverly conducted behind the scenes so that it is more difficult to see the actual situation of its victimization than ever before. In the border area where the flow of people is unceasing, trafficked victims are still lost in the waves of people crossing the border. This chapter attempts to examine what constitutes the method of support to trafficked victims based on the actual state of human trafficking in the border area.

THE DECADE AFTER THE PREVIOUS RESEARCH AND CROSSING THE BORDER THROUGH THE INTERNATIONAL BORDER CHECK POINT IN POIPET

Cambodia approved the *Law on Suppression of Human Trafficking and Sexual Exploitation* in 2008.[1] Compared with the previous *Law on Suppression of Kidnapping, Trafficking and Exploitation of Human Persons* (1996) this law is considered more comprehensive in terms of the prevention of human trafficking, particularly in regard to the tightened penal regulations.[2] Under the revised regulations, brokers who are found guilty of committing these crimes are to be punished more severely. Recently the Cambodian government has put great effort into anti-human trafficking measures with the support from aid agencies/actors such as UN agencies and NGOs. For example, the government has devoted itself to developing educational programs across the country for border police, police officers, village leaders, and teachers with the aim of enlightening them about the risks of human trafficking. Following these actions taken by the government and international organizations, there has been a decrease in smuggling and human trafficking in the area of the International Border Check Point, the legal point of crossing the border from Poipet[3] to Thailand.

The strength of the border control is surely effective in the decline of human trafficking across the legal route. However, as irony would have it, new ways to cross the borders without passing through the legal checkpoints have sprung up. Now, a large number of overland routes connecting Cambodia to its neighboring countries exist. These routes are used with increasing frequency by smugglers, brokers, and others wishing to cross out of Cambodia into a neighboring country. From this point of view, the intensification of the border control alone seems insufficient to solve the fundamental problem.

The classic example of how human trafficking was undertaken in the past was as follows: brokers would deceive their targets from the very beginning of the discussions about migratory labor. The victims would be taken to a different place than they had been told and would be required to work in jobs which were not what they had expected. Maybe one day they would be fortunate enough to be rescued from their plight and placed in a shelter.

However, human trafficking has begun to take on a new character, becoming more complicated and more difficult to identify today than ever before. It is now more difficult to distinguish regular migratory labor from human trafficking in the disguise of migration. For those who have no other choice but to migrate as the only means of livelihood, the probability of being trafficked is higher than ever.

In actuality, there is no end to the cases where migrant workers are potentially exposed to legal vulnerability. In some cases, for example, migrant workers do not keep their work permits with them, but instead their employers have them. In other cases, migrants do not know how to apply for work permission in detail because the job was arranged by the broker. This sometimes leads to a condition of forced labor, since in either of these example cases, the workers are unable to produce any documentation that they can use to protect themselves legally.

There are several ways to cross the border between Thailand and Cambodia for Cambodian people. In crossing the border from Cambodia to Thailand through the legal route, Cambodians are obliged to produce any one of these official documents: a valid passport; a Border Pass[4] or Border Ticket issued by Cambodia, and an Entry Card[5] issued by Thailand. A Border Pass is an official document valid exclusively to specified places in Thailand. Only Cambodians living in the border areas adjoining Thailand are allowed to hold it. With a Border Pass, the holders have a legal right to stay in the designated area for up to seven days. If it is necessary to extend the term of stay, further permission must be applied for. The Entry Card is an official permit issued by the Thai Border Control, and is valid only for the Rong Klua Market. Only Cambodians are permitted to hold this card and the term of validity is six months. This Entry Card with the name *Immigration Card* costs 200 baht (in 2013).[6] And, it is necessary for Cambodians to buy the Border Ticket for 10 baht (in 2013)[7] on the Cambodian side when they go to the Rong Klua Market from Cambodia. The ticket is valid for one day, and they have to produce it at the border control. Each way of crossing the border constitutes a different category of the length of stay and the permitted area in which to stay.

Apart from working in the Rong Klua Market, Cambodians have to apply for official working permission in order to work in Thailand. However, obtaining this permission is difficult for Cambodians for a number of reasons.[8] First, it is a complicated and time-consuming procedure, built on a system of ex post facto confirmation. Secondly, brokers and employers often produce the necessary documents for the registration on behalf of the workers concerned, meaning that the workers themselves are not involved in the process. Finally, it costs a large amount of money for Cambodian workers to acquire the legal status to work in Thailand. Many of the Cambodian workers the author interviewed did not know the details of the official working permit: some had never heard of the requirement for legal permission, and others knew that they had to apply for permission but had never seen the document themselves.

Even now, the majority of Cambodian workers have no legal right to work in Thailand, and they are exposed to the risks of either being arrested or deported to Cambodia. According to the material offered by the Poipet Transit Center,[9] the number of people deported from Thailand to Cambodia was 102,002 in calendar year 2012. Of these, 61,657 were men eighteen years old and older while the number of women in the same age category was 30,485. The number of boys under eighteen years of age was 5,765 and the number of girls was 4,095.[10]

Those who face deportation from Thailand because of undocumented entry are sent to the border gate at Poipet in a truck. Until it is possible to send a full truck-load of people back, those who are to be deported are kept in detention in Thailand. When the number of people reaches a full truck-load, they are sent back to Cambodia. These deportations are carried out an average of 152 times a month, with the highest number of times at 282 and the second highest at 203.[11]

In June 2014, the estimated number of legally unqualified migrants deported to Poipet ranged from 150,000 to 200,000 resulting in great confusion.[12] This is said to be partly because the then director of the National Council for Peace and Order (NCPO) of Thailand gave a warning that "Anyone who is involved in human trafficking and irregular migration, requiring legal registration of

Deportees Sent to the National Border in Poipet. *Source*: ©Yuko Shimazaki.

Source: ©Yuko Shimazaki.

foreign workers from their employers, should be punished."[13] At present, estimates of the number of Cambodians staying in Thailand for the purpose of working range from 700,000 to one million.[14]

OTHER ROUTES FOR CROSSING THE BORDERS WITHIN THE CORRIDOR

Although border controls have been intensified, human smuggling and human trafficking using informal routes to cross the border are on the rise. Moreover, many people now tend to use these.[15] Following this situation, Thailand began to issue the document called the Cambodian Working Permit.[16] This is part of the provisional measures taken by the Thai government to meet the urgent needs of Cambodians working in the immediate vicinity of the border. The document is issued under the jurisdiction of the Thai Border police, and its holders are allowed to work only in designated places in Thailand.[17]

At the border check point Cambodian workers are required to produce their permits and leave them with the Cambodian border police. After the permits are collected, the Cambodian border police submit them to the Thai border police as information about Cambodian migrants for the day. The Thai border police keep the documents until the Cambodian workers come back to the border and then they return them to the holders. Early in the morning they go to work crossing the border, and come back home in the evening. At the border gate, coils of barbed wire partition off the borders between Cambodia and Thailand. On the other side of the wire partition, their employers are waiting to take them to the workplace for the day.

Not all the Cambodian migrants possess a working permit. If someone fails to produce it at the border check point, the response from the border police of both nations depends on conditions. At present there seems to be no consistency in the formalities for entry at the border check point, so it is difficult to draw a clear distinction between what is legal and what is illegal. Because the Thai border guards keep the Working Permits until the workers return to the border at the end of the day, Cambodian migrants do not have anything that guarantees their legal status with them while working in Thailand. Except for the working permit, these migrants do not possess any other official working permit or identity card. The possession of the provisional working permit is effective in controlling the border but from the workers' point of view, if they do not hold it while working, it is useless for the purpose of securing the right to work and personal security. Therefore, without holding anything that protects their rights to work, Cambodian migrants working in Thailand remain exposed to legal vulnerability.

The reason Cambodians migrate to Thailand is because job openings are available on the other side of the border. Thailand, for its part, needs a workforce to fulfill the growing demand from farming and industries thriving in the areas close to the border. In response to the demand from Thailand, Cambodian migrants go to work, crossing the border as a matter of routine. Cambodian workers are substantially vulnerable to the risk of being trafficked because they have no access to useful information for the sake of their personal security. Human smuggling and human trafficking are rampant, riding on the waves of migratory laborers.

Primarily, border control is an area where the governments concerned should intervene with national laws. However, Cambodian migrant workers are not always protected under the existing law, and in many cases they are exposed to legal insecurity without national support. There is often a shortage of total consistency in the way the police and the border control of both nations intervene in the legal protection for migrant workers. The circumstances in which migrant workers are involved can be affected by the political relations between the two nations. They are also subject to the arbitrary interpretations

Migratory Workers Receiving Instructions from the Border Guard at the Border Provisionally Opened. *Source*: ©Yuko Shimazaki.

of the situation made by the officers in charge at the border control. Thus, in many cases, migration by Cambodians carries the risk of being threatened by such uncertain factors. There is a likelihood that migratory workers would suddenly be detained for a long period of time. Cambodian migrants who go to work on the other side of the border are vulnerable in the sense that they have no means of protecting themselves against issues which arise from political unrest and the arbitrary power of the authorities.

AID AND SUPPORT IN THE BORDER
AREA AND ITS LIMITS

The border area is a place which attracts people from all parts of Cambodia. From this perspective, Poipet shows a high incidence of human trafficking. This section attempts to consider critically if there is any room for improvements in the actual situation of aid and social development programs conducted in the border area at present. Furthermore, it also attempts to examine what constitutes an ideal method, or an approach which encourages trafficked victims to achieve their economic and social independence accompanied by the development of self-help.

As mentioned earlier, Poipet plays an important part as the foothold of the southern economic corridor to the Greater Mekong Subregion. It also serves as a staging point connecting the rural parts of Cambodia with the Thai market. Designated as a special economic zone, it boasts a remarkable increase in the mobility of people. From now, the position of the southern economic corridor and its influence on the Greater Mekong Subregion will be deeply consolidated if regional economic cooperation in the border areas is tightened.[18]

Cambodia has made large efforts to develop its economy under a national economic policy of "trickle down" through regional economic cooperation. Cambodian economic growth depends on the growth of the other industrially advanced nations in the Greater Mekong Subregion. The economic policies concerning development are decided at the upper level of government. Cambodia has invested public and private capital from Official Development Assistance (ODA) to most of the foreign aid in its economic development. The government has taken control of promoting development in the top-down style.

Under the banner of "the narrowing the economic gap between the regions" and "the reduction of national poverty," a series of projects have been promoted with the aim of activating the economy of the Greater Mekong Subregion. Cambodia is part of it and promotes its development domestically. Its headquarters in Phnom Penh leads projects of improving the infrastructure of roads, harbor facilities, and electricity. To all outward appearances,

Phnom Penh with its high-rise buildings boasts its prosperity generated by redevelopment.

However, the disadvantages brought about by the development projects under the control of the Cambodian government need to be considered. In spite of the seeming advancement in such large cities as Phnom Penh, disparity between the urban areas and the rural areas is exacerbated by exclusively focusing on economic development. The remarkable economic gap creates an active flow of people from the rural parts to the urban parts. Similarly, people move from the less-developed Cambodia to the more advanced Thailand.[19] The mobility of people increases the risk of human trafficking targeting mainly the economically underprivileged. In the economic hierarchy of Cambodia, less well-off people have no other choice but to migrate as the only means of making their livelihood. The majority of them live in rural villages where few job openings are available. Needless to say, it is the marginalized people that are forced into migration.

At present, the southern economic corridor is under development, with a large amount of ODA injected as one of the main sources of capital. Large cities and groups with vested interests have the full benefit of prosperity derived from the development of the economic corridor. Nevertheless, economic progress is parallel to economic disparity: the wide income differences urge people in rural villages toward the border area, looking for jobs. Among these migrants, in particular, the socially vulnerable are highly prone to exposure to the risk of being trafficked. Unfortunately, a painful reality lies ahead of them: they might be sent off to be traded in the regional market as commercial items after their humanity has been disregarded.

Migration across national boundaries is accompanied by the risk of human trafficking. In the border area, without a clear distinction between what is legal and what is illegal, there are still many cases of infringement of human rights. The extension of support to trafficked victims used to be conducted under the leadership of international organizations. However, they changed course and left, leaving their responsibilities to the Cambodian government. For this reason, at the moment, the government takes action for anti-human trafficking in the border area. Still, it seems to be insufficient to prevent the problem from expanding further.

In Cambodia, international humanitarian assistance and ODA were mainly focused on social development during the time of national recovery from the Civil War and national poverty reduction. Later, Cambodia entered a different phase where the introduction of a market economy into Indochina took preference. As government policy, in order to build a strong economic infrastructure, Cambodia expressed the necessity for aid in the form of private investment as more preferable and suitable for its purpose.

The history of aid and support by Japan, one of the top donors to Cambodia, dates back to 1959 when the Japan-Cambodia Agreement on Economic and Technical Cooperation was concluded. At that time Japan started to commit to economic cooperation with the nations of Southeast Asia in the form of war reparations, but Cambodia renounced its claim to them. Instead, Japan offered grants to cover the improvement of infrastructure and social development such as mother-and-child healthcare. However, aid from Japan was discontinued when the Pol Pot regime was set up, and Cambodia fell into political turmoil following the outbreak of the Civil War.

After the conclusion of the Paris Peace Agreement in 1991, the Japanese government recommenced grant-aid from 1992 onward. The grants covered landmine clearance and road repair as part of human security. During the time when UNTAC provisionally governed the country, Japanese aid was also appropriated for peace construction such as monitoring the general election and establishing the legal system. Aid for national recovery was also added. In 1999, Cambodia contracted for ODA loans.

Recently the Japanese government has concentrated on its aid and support for the economic development of Cambodia, adopting "the economic growth of the Mekong River Basin" and "the reduction of regional disparities in economy" as its catchwords. The Mekong Japan Summit has been held since 2009, and Japan used the occasion to grant Cambodia huge ODA loans to build a strong industrial infrastructure of water resources observation, road repair, harbor facilities, electricity, and communications. In cooperation with the Asian Development Bank (ADB), the Japanese government places more weight on investment in urban redevelopment and the improvement in infrastructure of special economic zones, which are expected to lay the groundwork for attracting private investment. Probably the Japanese government intended to offer "strategic aid," with the outlook of China's advancement into the region, and it can be safely said that Japan has drawn the rough outline of the economic development of Cambodia as presented today.

Japanese foreign aid to Cambodia was more conscious of the protection of human rights and the environment when it released the ODA Charter of 1992 and the Review of the ODA Charter of 2003. Nonetheless, Japan adopted the Development Cooperation Charter in 2015 and shifted its course toward giving priority to securing its national interests.

Following the vigorous economic growth of the Mekong River basin, a rapid increase in the number of people coming into the region can be clearly seen. These people are the economically needy and are attracted to ample job openings available in the region. Economic development demands priority, however, and the protection of the human rights of the vulnerable is considered to be of secondary importance. Therefore, the existing support system needs to be reconsidered, an assignment for the future to be tackled. In social development, the perspective of human rights has to be taken into consideration so as to secure the safety of the living environment for the vulnerable people who are left behind in economic progress. In terms of humanity, foreign aid ideally should be appropriated for building support systems that provide the socially vulnerable with more choices for making their livelihood. With more opportunities in life open to them, the possibility of achieving their financial independence will be enhanced.

In Poipet, aid programs have been conducted mainly in the form of emergency humanitarian assistance in response to the historical course of events which developed in the area. Several examples are: emergency relief for the essentials of food, clothing and housing to sustain human existence; dealing with the concerns of human rights, which are frequently recognized in the border area; protecting trafficked victims and deported persons, and sending them back to their home places. So far aid agencies/actors have taken the initiative in offering support to those who need it. However, as far as the present situation is concerned, there seems to be no clear indication of improvement. There are several reasons.

First, there has been a conspicuous increase in the flow of people into the border area. Donor country policies concerning foreign aid provide the background in terms of regional economic cooperation. Donor countries including Japan and the countries adjacent to Cambodia place more weight on the border economic growth and many people migrate to border areas from the rural areas. Because of such an increase in the mobility of people, on one hand, it makes it difficult for the administration to grasp the actual situation. On the other hand, aid agencies are kept busy attending to emergency cases one after another. As they have to stay within their budgets and with a fixed number of personnel, the present conditions do not allow them to cover all the needs.

Secondly, it is difficult for the humanitarian assistance, emergency support and other practical programs to guarantee all people a means of livelihood after the support program is finished. This is partly because the existing support programs generally lack long-term or even medium-term plans in the border areas. On the whole, the programs for trafficked victims and deported persons center chiefly on returning them to their home places after provisional assistance. However, among these people, for some returning home is not an option and so they have to remain in the area. The support programs found today are able to fulfill the basic needs of people, providing them with food, medical care, education, and housing. Nonetheless, after this provisional support is finished, the majority of the people are left without any means of earning their livelihood. Thus, in many cases, they are faced with the same situation as before, a situation where they are suffering in poverty. Because they are likely to migrate again to make a living—often at the the risk of being trafficked—emergency support might one day be necessary again. Economic independence acts as a shield against the victimization of human trafficking. It is therefore desirable that the aid agencies provide long-range programs until the people who need support find a source of livelihood.

The environmental conditions of the border area bring about another problem having an effect on the economic independence of the people. On the Cambodian side of this area, the plots allotted for residence are not suitable for farming as they would be in the rural village. Only a few people own farm plots—farming and raising chickens—because arable plots are limited. The rest of the people live a modest and simple life in a small hut on the lot given to them. These people are vulnerable to being victimized not only by human trafficking but also by human smuggling, both of which are frequently committed in the border area. Even if they own a house, without a source of income, the goal of achieving economic independence is still far off. A staff member of a local NGO worrying about the situation says that "we provide them with vocational programs in order for them to learn skills for their future career. But it takes a long time until they are trained in a skill. So, many of them choose to take up migration again after all."[20]

Support and assistance programs do not match what people in vulnerable situations expected to have from a practical point of view. It can be said that this discrepancy creates an environment where poverty is reproduced. In this condition, the vulnerable are likely to be victimized in human trafficking and other crimes. Although assistance programs are only able to provide just a part of people's needs, some people can enjoy the benefits. However, the problem is that among the people are those who suffer not only from deep poverty but also from other problems. In these cases, prior to receiving emergency assistance, it is advisable that they receive caring support for other concerns in addition to fulfilling the basic needs. For those who have finished with the support programs, ideally an environment should be provided in which they can seek support and advice until they will be able to gain the means of earning their livelihood. The reality is that the existing system has little effect on sustainability because it is lacking an uninterrupted support program. Taking this into consideration, the support systems should be reconsidered and reorganized into something more comprehensive and with additional stages.

The support systems found today in the border area employ a top-down style, and this one-sided approach, without involvement in their social environment leaves little room for the people's own choices. The people who need these support programs need also to abandon their passive attitudes, because this likely leads to a situation where their human rights are violated and they are lowered to the status of a mere object. When they are conscious of their situation, they can break a path through to establish their own capability. Once they are awakened to the meaning of self-reliance, they can be more positively concerned with social participation. Their active social engagement brings more opportunities and choices in life to them. Eventually, such a positive chain reaction generates a driving force in forming a community, which will be built on the foundation of aid agencies' support. Primarily, the assistance is a catalyst that gives people the chance to change social relations. It is the external intervention they encounter and the social environment they live in that determines whether the vulnerable are able to be set free from poverty or not.

SUMMARY

Reconsideration of Aid and Support in the Border Area

Surveys show that, in recent years, human trafficking has been in decline in Poipet, owing to the strength of border control. However, in fact, tightening of border controls has had a reverse effect: many migratory workers now cross the national borders through unofficial routes. Thus, in a legal sense, the personal security of these workers is threatened. The majority of workers are forced into labor on the other side of the border under unsettled and insecure working conditions. Crossing the border through these informal routes in itself is subject to constant uncertainty under conditions which are highly likely to be influenced by the political relations between Cambodia and Thailand. Considering this, workers crossing the border routinely are accordingly exposed to an unpredictable political situation.

Poipet is a stunning example of today's globalized market economy: Cambodian workers migrate for the purpose of earning cash income, and this workforce lays the groundwork not only for the prosperity of the Thai market but also for that of the regional and world market. Workers from Cambodia have vitally contributed to the economic growth of Thailand but in an inconspicuous way. In addition, they have played an important role in activating the market economy of the Mekong River basin. The inflow of capital into Cambodia accelerates the pace of its economic growth and that of expanding its market. This, in turn, creates a flow of people from rural villages into the border area, and broadly from Poi Pet into Thailand.

The dynamics fueled by this moving stream of people give a picture of the markets of the Mekong River basin and the world rising high over the other side of Poipet. These globally connected markets have their rise in the profit-seeking economy developed in the border area. The vulnerable, in particular women and girls, under the risk of being trafficked, have already been a part of this global business as profitable commercial items to be traded.

In the border area, people with a risk of being trafficked or smuggled live in a social environment where they suffer the bitterest poverty at the limit of the sustenance of life, and organizational suppor offered to meet their basic needs. With the flow of people uninterrupted, there are inevitably many people who fail to receive the necessary support. As a result, the peace and stability of the area are unavoidably uneasy. This disturbed state helps to create an environment in which poverty is reproduced: it makes the vulnerable more vulnerable to the risk of being victimized by crimes and further poverty. This being the case, external intervention serves little effect in sustainable improvement of recipients' living conditions because it does nothing more than provide provisional emergency assistance.

The existing support system in the area relies on "pushing back," which concerns itself in sending the people who are provided support back home after extending assistance necessary at the time. This one-way type of support should be reconsidered because it has little scope for considering the people's social conditions. By definition, emergency humanitarian assistance works for the sustenance of life. Overall, support systems consist of three parts: emergency assistance, support for self-help, and sustainable support. In the case of the border area at Poipet emergency assistance needs to be carried out in connection with the other two pillars of support, assistance for self-help and sustainability.

At the same time, the vulnerable themselves need to make efforts to overcome the state of being objectified and cultivate self-reliance. This works in parallel with forming a community based on deep mutual respect, which is built on each member's independence and communal spaces open to everyone. When they face up to an oppressive social structure and start to reorganize it into a more humane one, the vulnerable will seize the opportunity to liberate themselves from the poverty trap.

NOTES

1. NS/RKM/0208/005, in the PROMULGATES, it mentions that "The Law on Suppression of Human Trafficking and Sexual Exploitation that was passed by the National Assembly on 20 December 2007 during its 7th session of the 3rd legislature, and approved in its entirety by the Senate on 18 January 2008."

https://www.ilo.org/dyn/natlex/docs/ELECTRONIC/93355/109099/F-410 631367/KHM93355%20Eng.pdf, (Unofficial Translation: 03/03/08 by UNICEF).

2. Law on Suppression of Kidnapping, Trafficking and Exploitation of Human Persons (KHM-1996-L-59890), (The Khmer version is the official version of this document).

https://www.ilo.org/dyn/natlex/docs/ELECTRONIC/59890/60877/F65566
6645/KHM59890%20English.pdf.

3. Poipet formerly was registered as a Commune (in Khmer/Cambodian language, Khum) belonging to the district (in Khmer, Srok). Because of population increase and the influence of its designation as a Special Economic Zone, in December 2008, Poipet was changed from a Commune, the subdivision of a district, to Municipality. Poipet was integrated into its neighbor, Nimit Commune, as a municipality (Krong Paoy Paet) during the period from 12th January 2008 to 9th January 2009, and it was officially organized as an independent administrative municipality. Staff of the Ministry of Social Affairs, Veterans and Youth Rehabilitation (MoSVY) in Poipet office and NGO members working in Poipet in 2013 confirmed this point when interviewed.

4. The border pass is similar to a passport in size and content.

5. The Card for Cambodian people, named the *Immigration Card*, by Sakeao Immigration under Thai Government. The Immigration Card notes name, nationality, occupation, age, height, gender, and day of issue/day of expiration. The author researched this in 2012 and 2013.

6. Interviews with villagers, NGOs, and MoSVY staff in Poipet in February 2012 and August 2013.

7. Interviews with daily workers, NGOs, and MoSVY staff in Poipet in February 2012 and August 2013.

8. Interviews with NGO members who were helping the deportees, forced labor migrants, and victims of human trafficking in Poipet, Battambang, Phnom Penh in 2012–2016.

9. The data was provided by Ministry of Social Affairs Veterans and Youth Rehabilitation (MoSVY) in Poipet office on August 14, 2013.

10. The numbers cited in the text includes boys and girls accompanied by their family members. The data from MoSVY does not indicate whether those who have been deported are victims of human trafficking or not. This data also does not indicate personal details such as gender.

11. In deportation from Thailand, Poipet is designated to accept deported persons and a team of organizations concerned works together to take care of deported people. The team is formed by MoSVY, the Border Control of Cambodia, international organizations, and NGOs. The base in Poipet, also known as the Transit Center, operates a system for providing protection provisionally for trafficked victims, when victims of human trafficking are found among deported persons. In this case, the Center makes contact with NGOs calling for support, after protecting victims (at present, the Center is chiefly operated by the Cambodian government after the responsibility was transferred from the international organizations concerned). In other border areas, there is neither a center run by organizations in cooperation nor a transit center. As of March 2013, owing to the shrinkage of the national budget and that of the international organizations concerned, there was a decline in operations by the organizations in cooperation and functions by the Transit Center. As the number of deported persons is on the rise, the Kamrieng border gate, the province of Battambang, was designated to deal with deportation in addition to Poipet. According to the local newspaper issued in Cambodia called, *Koh Setepheap*, on February 28, 2017, the early dawn edition, 315 persons were sent to the border gate on the grounds that they had no legal right to stay. As of April 2019, the transit center is at the Kamrieng border gate in Battambang province.

12. According to interviews with persons concerned in an NGO and those who had no legal right to stay in Thailand (August and September in 2014), among those who arrived at the border, there were those who were deported and those who returned voluntarily. They said that far more than ten thousand people crowded at the border in a single day at the time. Among the workers whom the author interviewed then, some did not know that they had no legal qualification to stay until this incident took place. One reason for this was that workers had brokers to arrange everything necessary for their migration, paying a commission for it (from the interviews taken in September in 2014).

13. NCPO denied ever having excluded Cambodian workers forcibly and emphasized that the incident was caused by a rumor that swept through the country. According to the interviews with the returnees at that time, many said something similar to: "Three days before coming back to Cambodia, the police came to the place I lived in Thailand and told me to go back to Cambodia or I would be arrested. Then I was scared and came back home" (in September 2014).

14. Interview with the director of the Poipet Transit Center in August 14, 2013.

15. Field research from 2011 to 2019. And also NGO staff in Poipet, Battambang, Phnom Pen mentioned the same point in interviews. One staff of an NGO said, "There are so many unofficial routes and over 100 corridors in Poipet" (interviewed February 8, 2012 in Poipet).

16. Prery Kup Border (in August 2013). On the basis of the interviews with the Cambodian Border police and the residents who possessed the working permit, applications for the permits were accepted around May 2013. In the working permit (its heading written as *The Cambodian Working Permit*), the items to be filled out were as follows: enter the country in the morning and leave in the evening; the course; address in Thailand (the names of Province, County, Administrative District, and Village); age; gender; facial photograph; and the address in Cambodia. There is no reference to the jurisdiction of administrative offices concerned in the issue of the certificate. According to the Poipet Border police, only the residents of the specified village were allowed to hold it. The interviews conducted in August 2013 indicated that there was a divergence of information regarding the cost of applying for the permit and the conditions for acquiring it, and so on.

17. Working is permitted in the designated place only: Pa Rai Mai village, Pa Rai subdistrict, Aranyaprathet district, Sa Kaeo province in Thailand (as of August in 2013).

18. Northern sub-corridor route of Greater Mekong Subregion Southern Economic Corridor (SEC) is Bangkok—Poipet (Paoy Paet)—Sisophon (Serei Saophoan)—Siem Reap—Stung Treng—Rathanakiri—Ou Yadav—Pleiku. It is along National Highways No. 6 and No. 64 in Cambodia (ADB, Review of Configuration of the Greater Mekong Subregion Economic Corridors, 2016). http://documents1.worldba nk.org/curated/en/580101540583913800/pdf/127247-REVISED-CambodiaUrbaniza tionReportEnfinal.pdf.

19. The Comparable monthly wage in Phnom Penh is US$201 and in Bangkok US$413, https://whttps://www.bk.mufg.jp/report/insasean/AW20190508.pdf.

20. Interview with NGO in Poipet on August 12, 2013.

Chapter 6

How to Break Away from the Vicious Circle of Poverty

In human trafficking, generally speaking, the majority of victims are socially vulnerable people. An understanding of the victimization of human trafficking needs to consider the victims' family situations and the backgrounds of their family members. This chapter attempts to examine the process of how the trafficked women including their family members made efforts to break away from the vicious circle of poverty. The factors encouraging them to bring a halt to the negative cycle of poverty are: appropriate support from NGOs, information about social skills, and sympathetic attitudes of the people around them. Based on these factors, this chapter also attempts to illustrate the path by which the trafficked women have grown into independent individuals. These women broke through a path to set themselves free from the poverty trap with help from supporting organizations. In the process of gaining their independence, they developed a sense of self-direction and learned to act on their own initiative. Their forward-looking attitude brought about changes in the present social environment.

THE GROWTH OF THE VULNERABLE INTO INDEPENDENT INDIVIDUALS

Case Study: Som

Family situation: Som, eighteen-year-old daughter, fourteen-year-old son, and eleven-year-old daughter

HIV Infection and Subsequent Discrimination

After her husband's death, Som felt something unusual in her health. She had a blood test at a health center run by an NGO and discovered that she was infected with HIV. When she came to know that she was HIV-positive, she was at a total loss about what she could do for the future. She was so sad about such a deplorable situation that she could not help crying every single day. Som lost weight day by day and felt languid. Some of her neighbors were worried about her and paid her visits, wondering what was wrong with her health. However, when she told them that she was infected with HIV, the neighbors suddenly changed their attitude toward her and stopped visiting her. No one talked to her any more. Her children were abandoned by their friends and isolated in the village. At that time people who were HIV-positive were discriminated against because there was as yet no precise knowledge and correct information about HIV/AIDS.

The Economic Conditions of Som's Family

Som used to grow vegetables on a part of the land owned by her sister-in-law, and sold them. Now that the neighbors knew that she was infected with HIV, nobody bought vegetables from her. Her neighbors displayed overt acts of discrimination and prejudice towards living with those who were HIV-positive. Having no other choice, she barely made a living by selling vegetables to a dealer, and gaining cash income from it. When she needed more cash, she had to borrow money to feed her children.

The Migration by Som's Children

When Som was in bed feeling ill, brokers visited her one after another. They made proposals that she should send her children to work, for example, in Poipet or in Thailand. For days, Som worried about whether she would send them or not. The brokers who would visit her gave her some rice and other food. Pretending to care about her children, they urged her to allow her children to migrate. Under these circumstances, Som had no friend to talk to and could not think of any possible alternatives. Worse, the economic conditions of Som's family became even more severe. Although the brokers did not provide Som with any exact information about the details of her childrens' migration, the plan for them to migrate to Thailand moved forward. She said that her uneasiness deepened because she was left out of it.

The Days When She Went through Discrimination
and Joined a Self-Help Group

At that time, the village leader noticed that Som's children were exposed to the risk of human trafficking on the grounds that Som was in a tight economic situation and brokers were visiting her. The leader went to a local NGO and told them about her situation. The NGO put her name on the priority support list soon after they confirmed the situation. On this occasion, Som became a member of a self-help group run by the NGO as a part of its support programs.

She participated in the workshop primarily because she was given medicine for HIV, daily commodities, and food by the NGO. In addition, she counted on the prospect that her children would be looked after properly. She thought that there was no better opportunity than this. At that time, Som and her children were in a desperate situation, which she put in her own words as, "If we had done nothing my children and I would have died from hunger." She decided to join the self-help group as the only way to solve this predicament.

Her Participation in the Program and Her Attitude toward Others

Before she joined the life-support program, she felt isolated in the village. However, now that she was a member of the program, she met other people for the first time who were in a socially deprived environment and were going through the same situation as she was. She expressed her feelings thus:

> I am not the only one who has had hard times. When I started to go to the workshop in the NGO, I felt my loneliness was gone. Before I came here, I had no friend to talk to, but not now. I can talk to the group members about my problems openly. This makes me so happy. One more thing, I feel far less lonely than before. Instead, I feel better now. I think my life has definitely turned for the better too.

Som participated in the program actively, and she was in better health. She had a better understanding of those who were in the same situation as hers. Out of sympathy for their plight, she voluntarily visited other people who did not participate in the program. Now, as a group leader, Som takes the initiative to visit people in the same situation as she was before. She makes this effort not only to let them know about the NGO's life-support program but also to keep needy families from isolation in the community.

As a Group Leader

Poor and needy families in the village were discriminated against on the grounds of their poverty. They were isolated not only from society but also from access to information. Until Som called on them, their human relationships were also extremely poor. It was all they could do to feed their children and maintain a daily living. However, they too joined the program and self-help group because of Som's visits. They told her that they felt much less isolation than before. Som was encouraged by the positive feedback from them. Now she finds her work rewarding and worth doing.

Looking back at her life, she said that

> I have neither thought of a day like this nor have I thought of myself engaging in such an activity. But now, I feel I can do something to help people. I am really encouraged when I think of someone waiting for me. In the activity of the self-help group, every one of us can talk about whatever problem we have. We can share a sense of solidarity with each other, and this makes us feel we are not alone anymore.

Som has enthusiastically taken up the role assigned to her as a group leader and now works for the NGO. She thought that if she had not encountered the NGO, she and her children would have been trafficked and forced into labor.

Change in the Social Environment

Som and others in a socially vulnerable position now take action in educating neighbors about their actual situation. Their intention is to give precise and correct information because incorrect information is highly likely to lead to intensified discrimination and prejudice against the needy. At first, the neighbors became confused and embarrassed about their activity. However, gradually they showed a better understanding of vulnerable people and gained a positive attitude toward them. The regional community in itself is now showing some signs of improvement.

Som said that "I have never thought that the role I took on would bring a life like this. This is totally different from the life I had lived before I met the NGO. We are in the same boat. We are not alone. Now I am confident in myself because now I am assigned a role to perform."

At the moment, Som visits a total of twenty-eight families regularly and asks after them. The families she visits are fatherless families, poor families with a high risk of human trafficking, and a widow whose husband died from AIDS. Prior to Som's visits, they used to be isolated in the village because of discrimination against their poverty, and they used to be frightened of their neighbors and kept them at a distance.

The Intervention of External Support and Peer Supporters

After her husband died, Som became a single mother. Som was economically underprivileged, as well as infected with HIV. Discrimination and prejudice forced her into isolation in the village. Som's case is typical of a socially vulnerable family, which accidentally becomes a family victimized by human trafficking. Som had difficulties feeding her family and her own health declined. She could find no means of living, and she was totally at a loss about the future. At that time, she considered the migration of her young children as the only means of living left for her.

Som was not alone in saying, "There is no food at all"; "There is nothing we can do"; and "We would have been dead, if nothing could have been done." Other vulnerable people were also at the limits of their existence, and they could not find the strength to hold out any longer. These families were in severe economic conditions, so they were highly susceptible to human trafficking. When Som was in a hopeless plight, staff members of the NGO visited her and invited her to their support program and self-help program. The intervention of the NGO gave her the chance to change her life. In her case, the village leader was the key person who monitored the state of affairs in the village. It was he who afforded her the chance to have contact with the NGO. Thanks to him in large measure, a social network was set up between the NGO and the village.

Som expressed her feelings toward the NGO staff members by saying "When I was isolated, they came to see me many times, and that made me feel so happy. They were concerned about us and explained the activities and programs they had for us. To be honest, they would give us food for tomorrow, and that was the most important thing for me."

"I was much relived to know that our daily lives would be guaranteed by someone outside caring about us," Som explained. Her prime objective in having a connection with the NGO was to "have food for the day" and to "have support for her life." Although at first, she just expected just food and support for life from the NGO, her repeated participation in the program eventually led her to discover that it was far better than she could have imagined at the beginning. Now she thought that her life had changed positively in many ways.

This is probably attributable to the fact that she met people in the same situation as hers and built good relationships with them. She mentioned that "I had never thought of anyone in the same circumstances as mine." She was much relieved to know that there were other people in the same living conditions.

Because of their participation in the NGO self-help group, Som and other members mentioned that (table 6.1): "I was able to build up my strength thanks to my peer supporters" (sixteen persons); "My supporters' presence makes me feel confident" (thirteen); "Now I have the will to live" (eleven); "I feel I can take an initiative in controlling things in my life" (five). They found positive changes in themselves.[1] Although they used to be pessimistic about the future, their internal changes brought about corresponding effects in

Table 6.1   **Changes in the Minds of the Participants in the Self-Help Group**

The Internal Changes (multiple answers)	The Number of People
I have the will to live	11
I am able to build up my strength thanks to my peer supporters	16
I have my role to take on	4
I have friends	10
The presence of my peer supporters makes me feel confident	13
I am able to speak in the presence of people	3
I came to know how to protect myself	3
I have the will to work	4
I feel more secure in leading my daily life	3
I can make plans for the future	2
I can take my initiative in control things in my life	5
No change	2
Total	76

their views of life. Now they take an affirmative and positive attitude toward their lives.

In the past, Som could not talk to anyone about her personal problems. However, now that she has gained friends in the self-help group run by the NGO, she can talk to them frankly about her concerns. After spending some time with the group members, she has developed the idea that "we have a far better understanding of each other because we live in the same circumstances." Sharing sympathy with each other, she enjoys a sense of unity and group solidarity.

Until joining the NGO's program these people, including Som, never had the chance to know anyone in the same situation. However, joining the self-help group in the NGO allowed them to know each other through discussing their problems openly and supporting each other. Thereby, they now share a sense of oneness with each of the members. Their engagement with the workshop shows the formation of a new type of community. This is not a hierarchal community but a community where members are treated fairly and support each other equally. Through a series of actions, these women have brought changes in the social environment in which they live.

From a Target of the Program to a Peer Supporter

Som was initially a target of the NGO program, but eventually she became a provider of support to others who needed it. This change in her role shows that the key factor lies in the formation of a place where vulnerable women and those at a high risk of trafficking can gather together. There they are open to discussion of their problems with the other group members. Over a period of time, they become aware that the other members are also directly involved in poverty and are also in socially marginalized positions. They can express their sympathy for each other, and they are confident in showing and getting a better understanding of each member.

Once a target of the NGO's attention but now with a role as a group leader, Som has the initiative in leading the group activities and offers support to those who need it. She cares for every one of the group members, showing her understanding of the situations in which each lives. Her actions give her the opportunity to grow in self-confidence. As a result, she can now rely on her own efforts and abilities to solve her problems in a far better way than before. At the same time, her thoughtful approach to the group makes the members more closely united with each other. Mutual care and support among the members allow them to build good relationships. The corresponding effect is the formation of a community which attaches importance to mutual help.

Som explains the change in her position from a target of the program as an aid recipient to a peer supporter as, "I think I understand their feelings in a better way, because I used to be given support. Then I realized I could do something for them. I also wondered if there is anyone in the same position as I was before." She was highly motivated to make use of her own experiences in working for people in the same situation as she had been in. Moreover, she had self-direction for considering others and making a contribution to helping them.

Along with Som, others have also grown from aid/program recipient/ participant to peer supporter in the NGOs, volunteering to take on a role as group leader. Asked about why they were willing to take on leadership roles, they answered, "This was because the words from friends were a great encouragement to me" and "A strong feeling that I can do something arose in myself."

The gradual development of self-direction within the vulnerable involves acting on their own initiative in support of others. This action brings a spontaneous change, and it leads to a further maturity in them. This can be described as the positive chain reaction in which the result of the previous experience causes a corresponding positive effect in the following experience. This is the opposite to the negative circle of poverty. It also explains the process of how the vulnerable overcome their problems with poverty. The process is accompanied by the awakening of self-direction within them. As they further develop this sense of self-direction, they become more actively engaged in support activities, showing their sympathy and care for others. The relationships among them grow into relationships built and based on unity. In this process, the positive cycle, or the virtuous circle, has already begun, and it produces a sure sign that a new type of community is going to be created.

These peer supporters used to be targets of the program as supported persons who themselves went through tight economic situations at the risk of health and life. At present, they are engaged in helping people in the same situation as theirs. When they see some positive change in the recipients' view of life, they feel joy and a sense of fulfillment as a supporter. They remark, "I am so happy to be a support"; "Now I know I can be of a support to others"; "By taking on a role to perform, I am more confident in myself"; and "I am more conscious of my membership in the group in a positive sense." What they achieve is not just a feeling of joy but also, surely, a boost in self-respect. Furthermore, these positive feelings improve the sense of oneness between supporters and recipients.

From this point of view, helping and supporting the needy is a social activity. At first, a supporter serves in-between a recipient and the supporting program. In this way the recipient has the opportunity to join the program through the intervention of the supporter. At this point, however, there is no personal contact established between a supporter and an aid recipient yet. After a period of time has passed, through sharing problems with each other and working on them together, the aid recipient shows signs of improvement and has a positive attitude. Closer contact with the recipient also effectively generates an internal change in the mind of the supporter. When they enter into the feelings of each other, both of them experience a positive emotional effect.

Moreover, the initial participation in support programs by the needy works as a catalyst for reestablishing the openness of the rural village. This is realized when the vulnerable gradually expand the scope of their activity through their contact with society. Regaining openness suggests the creation of a community, which should be open to everyone. It also means the replacement of an authoritarian community with a community open to people of different interests, regardless of social classes. This is partly because an authoritarian community has a general tendency to marginalize the vulnerable and outsiders.

An open community serves to build a new social structure which does not cause such negative factors as poverty and the marginalization of the vulnerable. Rebuilding the social structure starts with a minor alteration in social relations between the members of the village community. Hand-in-hand with the rebuilding of the community is the growth of a social movement based on relationships between individuals on a village-wide scale. As the social movement develops to a further stage, it gradually exerts influence on the whole society.

For instance, when vulnerable individuals are engaged in social activity in a village, it could change the opinions held by other villagers about them. At the sight of their commitment to social participation, some village members might think that "they can do it" and "they were thought to be irrelevant to social work. But their efforts now bear fruit." They are the people who used to be made targets of discrimination and prejudice. However, their efforts successfully earn them positive response from other villagers. In developing social contact with others, they experience a spontaneous change in themselves. Although they were labeled as vulnerable at the beginning, there are improvements not only with the previous attitude of the villagers toward them but also in the relationships between them. In due course, the positive effect extends to include the social relations operating in the village.

As the case of Som shows, the initial minor change produces a positive chain reaction in social relations and in the social environment. When the relationship between Som and the others around her partly changed, it contributed to making the social environment in which she lived far better. In time, it led to the formation of a communal network in the village where she lived. This is a communal network for those who need help and support. Behind this successful example, there is a village community which attaches much importance to mutual support. This network is built on the model of the Cambodian rural village. In general, the rural village in Cambodia enjoys a system of mutual support. Close contact with neighbors and reciprocal help lay the foundation for the social environment of the rural village. Had it not been for the background knowledge of the rural village where members share a sense of unity with each other, there would not have been the formation of a regional community as such.

On the other hand, Cambodian rural villages tend to adopt an authoritarian approach and put their members under control. Thus it can be said that the rural community in Cambodia has two opposite aspects. However, when community members work on social improvement through their active social participation, such negative aspect of the rural community can be diminished. As Som's case shows, efforts made by the people will be able to reverse authoritarian and exclusionary aspects in favor of generosity and openness.

THE PROCESS OF ACHIEVING INDEPENDENCE BY A VULNERABLE WOMAN

The Process of Independence

For the vulnerable, how to stop the negative cycle of poverty is one of the most pressing matters to consider. It attaches the highest importance to developing a sense of self-direction. The first step for the development of self-direction is considering what one can be and what one can do. As they enlarge the range of activity and the scope of capability, the quality of life of the vulnerable can be improved further. In making improvements in life, it is necessary to strengthen the entitlement of human rights, the participation of individuals in social life, and the enhancement of self-respect. Basic human rights—the right to existence, including the right to food, clothing, and housing—along with social and cultural rights, are the basic factors which form the foundation for improving the quality of life. In a broad sense, the state of poverty can be described as a state caused by the shortage of any one of these factors. From this point of view, it is vitally important for the vulnerable to develop a sense of direction so as to set themselves free from the trap of poverty. When they start to act by relying on their own efforts to control things, instead of depending on other people for instruction, the possibility of liberating themselves from poverty opens up before them.

In this book, the vulnerable are defined as people who are forced into passivity in society. As the example cited earlier in the text shows, even though they are sometimes be treated as mere objects within the existing social structure, in actuality the vulnerable hold the possibility of cultivating a sense of self-direction. If given support from NGOs and a communal network, they are able to build social relations through contact with other vulnerable people. Figure 6.1 explains the process of improving the social environment in which vulnerable women live.

Som. *Source*: ©Yuko Shimazaki.

< Change >   < Relationship with Outsiders>

Difficulty in maintaining one's existence   Dependent on the external environment

An external intervention (NGOs, etc): to   ◄── ① ──►   Having self- awareness
know other people in the same situation   and self- recognition

Contact with others: listening to them and   ◄── ② ──►   Having perspective for oneself: boosting
articulating one's own problems   self-respect

Longing for self-direction/independence and ◄── ③ ──►   Taking a look at the external environment
self-confidence   relatively: the expansion of capabilities

Sympathy and unity with the people in the   ◄── ④ ──►   Generating a social power to change social
same situation   environment for the better

Finding one's own individuality: Establishing one's identity:
development of self-motivation   restoring and protection of human rights

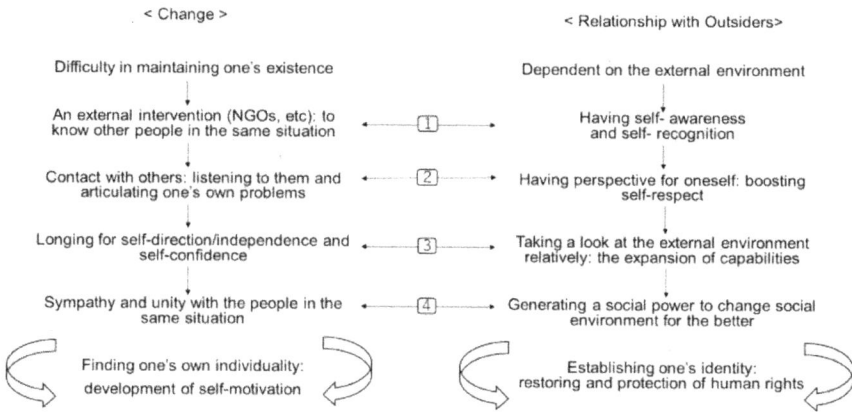

Figure 6.1   Changing Stages of the Vulnerable.

At first, the vulnerable are likely to be influenced negatively by the existing social structure and placed in a position with less power in a hierarchal society. Within the existing society they are treated as an objectified being with a lack of self-direction. As a whole, the vulnerable are in a state of poverty. Moreover, they are caught in a negative chain reaction. This is triggered by such factors as poverty, the loss of property, the separation of family, and the isolation caused by discrimination and prejudice. Some of them live in multidimensional poverty complicated by several factors working interconnectedly. The intervention of supporting organizations is carried out at this point. They have difficulty in maintaining their existence and are dependent on the external environment.

Through support from organizations, as the first sign, the vulnerable gradually feel the dawn of self-awareness. Before receiving support, it was all they could do to feed themselves, or perhaps, even, it was difficult for them to get food for the day. They were so occupied with domestic worries that they had almost no chance to care for themselves. But on the occasion when they have contact with other people, they are able to find a new perspective for self-recognition. Social contact with others in the similar situation creates an internal change. The presence of others works as a mirror, permitting them to see who they are in a different light. It allows them to know that they are not the only ones who suffer from poverty, and it helps greatly in the alleviation of the feeling of isolation. Eventually, they hold a sense of security and feel more relieved than before. Their contact with others marks the beginning of a new phase in their self-recognition.

In the second stage, they start to look at themselves more closely and feel the awakening of self-respect. In the place where the underprivileged gather together, they can discuss their personal problems. When they listen to other people talking about their problems openly, they reflect on themselves thinking, "This person is in the same situation as mine, but she has more difficult problems in this regard"; "I am faced with a more challenging situation than hers"; and "This person has another problem in addition to the matter she is now talking about." They are at the phase where they reach self-knowledge through making comparisons between themselves and others. By looking at themselves consciously, they realize that they are in an underprivileged position and treated as less important in society. To restore their human rights is a challenging task assigned to themselves so as not to remain treated as marginalized beings.

When they learn to see themselves in a different perspective, they come to know what kinds of problems they have. By analyzing the reasons for their problems, they begin to try to find solutions to their present situation. Then, they learn to understand the position they occupy in family and social relations. By articulating their problems in the self-help group discussion, they can listen to others' opinions and seek advice if necessary. At the same time, receiving feedback from the other members, they can give the matters reconsideration. When they see someone listening to them carefully, a feeling of confidence grows in themselves. They used to be so slighted and treated as such that they had to oppress the feeling of self-worth.

In the third phase of changing themselves for the better, they set out to enlarge opportunities in life, and this is supported by developing a sense of self-direcction and confidence. They are then encouraged to cope with the situation by themselves. By acting in this way, they are able to develop a sense of self-direction. This indicates that they have become concerned with the question of what position they can place themselves within the existing society. At the very beginning, they were in circumstances which dictated that they had no other choice but to live in the social environment offered to them. In different terms, they had to resign themselves to a life of deep poverty. Nonetheless, they joined the self-help group and received vocational training. In the process of exploring the possibility of achieving their economic independence, they began to feel confidence growing in themselves.

Vulnerable women were denied educational opportunities because they lived not only in the conditions of economic poverty but also of relative poverty. For these educationally underprivileged, it is first of all important to have confidence in themselves with a belief in their own abilities. This is an essential precondition for setting them free from the lower position in the hierarchal society. It is self-confidence that helps them to enlarge their opportunities in life. It also inspires them to entertain a hope for tomorrow. Thus, they take a more positive attitude toward the future. They used to be so occupied with how to survive for the day that they could not afford to think of tomorrow. Now they are assured to step forward to lead a life of their own.

The fourth phase of changing themselves is concerned with sympathy. Vulnerable women start to develop sympathy for others, and it makes them feel more closely attached with each other. Furthermore, the solidified unity can be a driving force for changing the present social environment for the better. In Som's case, she was engaged in social activities more actively in the community when she improved her self-motivation. She voluntarily visited the families suffering from isolation and people in desperate need. She earnestly encouraged them to join the self-help group by letting them know "you are not alone." This was done out of her sincere sympathy for the people in isolation.

Sympathy has a power that makes changes in established community relationships between the wealthy and the needy. It also potentially helps to alter the minds of those who practice discrimination and display prejudice against poverty. This can be described as "social power." It works as a driving force for replacing traditional social relations with relations built on the basis of sympathy. In the newly created social relations, the economically deprived have a positive outlook of life, unlike in the days when they could hardly think of the future. Having gained a strong will to live well, they even enjoy making plans for tomorrow. Backed up by a positive view of life, they hew out a path of their own. In regaining and protecting the human rights of the vulnerable, establishing their individuality takes importance. With their human rights secured, the vulnerable can be transformed into independent individuals with human dignity.

The case of Som gives an example of how an economically vulnerable woman has developed a sense of self-direction and contributed to social improvement. At the beginning, the vulnerable were in circumstances in which they had no other choice but to resign themselves to the present condition. Although they were marginalized, by passing through several phases, they can become potential contributors to improving the existing social environment.

The Significance of Self-Awareness

As in the case of Som cited earlier, intervention, mainly by NGOs, encourages the vulnerable to develop self-direction. Through programs provided by NGOs, they learn to look at themselves closely, and they come to know what position they actually occupy. At this stage, they should learn not to resign themselves to the present situation but to understand it as something that is changeable through their own engagement and effort. This is the first step to break a new path to establishing their individuality.

The vulnerable are usually forced into silence and a passive role in social relations. However, they can be awakened to the significance of voluntary involvement in changing their living conditions through external intervention. In the process of developing a sense of self- awareness and independence, they learn to change their role from a passive one to an active one. This is an action that can be explained: "When the vulnerable start to articulate their thoughts and experiences and make them into a theory, they rise up for social change armed with the theory."[2]

If they remain separated from their own problems, the vulnerable cannot be aware of their own social position. As long as they are forced into passivity and silence in relation to the external environment, they cannot change anything concerned with their living conditions. When they realize the significance of self-awareness, they come to understand their reasons for existence as members of society. After they appreciate their membership in the present society, they can step forward toward changing society for the better, taking an active role in social relations.

Given that someone is faced with a severe situation, how much is the person to blame for what happened? For example, assume that there are two people in extreme poverty but one of them has not realized the significance of self-awareness yet, then this person would be passive against being poor without a perspective for self. Meanwhile, if the other person has already realized the significance of self-awareness, this person would have understood the meaning of poverty and taken some action for it. Both of them know very well that they suffer from poverty, but they are different in the way they understand the meaning of the situation they share.

Considering again that the vulnerable are faced with a severe situation, it matters whether they are aware of the meaning of solidarity or not. Without grasping the significance of solidarity, one cannot take responsibility for one's own situation. The vulnerable are in desperate poverty, so they cannot afford to think of themselves in a detached way. Therefore, they are to be supported materially and psychologically in an appropriate way. The vulnerable cannot be blamed for their poverty without taking the context into consideration. The problems which the vulnerable always face cannot be attributed to personal responsibility. With a lack of clear focus on oneself, it is quite difficult for the vulnerable not only to insist on their rights but also to establish their own entitlements.

After the vulnerable people have realized the significance of solidarity, they spontaneously show their sympathy toward other vulnerable people. This sympathy drives them to build a network in the community they live in, for the purpose of supporting each other. The network functions as a safety net for the vulnerable. Backed up by a system of mutual support, they can enlarge the range of their activity and the scope of their ability, accompanied by more choices and opportunities in life.

When the well-being of the vulnerable is improved, the unity of community members becomes correspondingly tighter. The closeness and openness in the community brings about change in the existing environment. In the sense that an improved social environment is a product of the unity of community members, a better environment for the vulnerable is a community in which mutual support systems function well enough to care for each of them. The well-being of the vulnerable can be guaranteed by the presence of a communal support system.

SUMMARY

The Path to Breaking Away from Poverty

In the long-run, the quality of support determines the quality of life for the vulnerable. In considering what support can be fruitful for needy people, the quality of support should be one that encourages the vulnerable to achieve social and economic independence with human dignity. In other words, support should not be offered without first grasping what problems the needy people have. Unilateral assistance is likely to prevent them from developing a sense of self-help. There is also a risk that such support perpetuates dependence. It is also incorrect to assume that the needy are to be blamed for their poverty. The problems they have cannot always be attributed to personal responsibility. Obviously, they are desperate for help in order to survive another day, but without appropriate support, they remain stuck in the poverty trap. They are left in circumstances in which they are deprived of the right to well-being.

In terms of human rights, it is necessary for the vulnerable to seek support, which encourages them to take an active role in social relations, once their basic needs of food, clothing, shelter, and personal security are met. The fulfillment of these basic needs allows them to stop being passive and move on to a further stage where the right to well-being is fulfilled. For supporters, it is important to take a role of helping the vulnerable in achieving their social and economic independence both materially and spiritually. Finally, for both the supporters and the vulnerable, it is desirable to develop a partnership so as to work together in changing unfair social relations to fair and meaningful ones.

As long as the vulnerable do not take action for achieving their independence, they have no other course but to remain dependent on external support. As far as the vulnerable are still exposed to social and economic vulnerability without the awareness of solidarity, it is actually quite challenging for them to regain their human rights. In this situation, the existing oppressive social structure will remain unchanged. In places where the vulnerable are denied their human rights and deprived of human dignity, the intensified societal pressure will keep them passive and marginalized.

However, when the vulnerable become aware of the significance of solidarity, it will be the first step to break a new path to develop society. Particularly, they need to be conscious of the present social conditions with which their problems are deeply connected. In changing society for the better, for recipients and supporters equally, and for those who exercise social influence and those who are influenced alike, it is necessary to adopt a critical attitude toward the present society to see if there is any room for improvement. Change on one side only cannot generate a driving force for a radical reconstruction of the social structure. When both sides work together hand-in-hand in changing themselves for the better, it effectively brings about a corresponding change in society and structure as well. This will be a society where each member makes an effort to form a peaceful society with a longing to reduce poverty.

NOTES

1. Interview in Battambang province on December 2007.
2. Shouji Nakanishi and Chizuko Ueno, *Toujisya syuken* [The Sovereignty of the Parties Concerned] (Tokyo: Iwanami Shoten, 2003).

Conclusion

It has already been sixteen years since my research on human trafficking in Cambodia was started. Under the banners of development, poverty alleviation, education, and human rights, numerous international organizations and NGOs gathered together in Cambodia from all over the world to offer international aid and assistance. To date, an enormous amount of money has been invested in the reconstruction of Cambodia and spent on aid and support for those who needed help. Now, the waves of international aid for social development projects have been gradually decreased or withdrawn. Instead, new waves of economic development and private investment have rolled in. At the moment, these words are heard in every corner of the country. On the surface of Cambodian society, the words "poverty" and "human rights" are not so often heard as before, as if they were obsolete. Nonetheless, poverty still exists in Cambodian society. Thus, it is necessary for today's international society to offer a steady gaze at the poverty left in obscure corners of Cambodian society. It is to be understood as an earnest warning against marginalizing the issue of poverty.

Cambodia has been greatly changed over the past decade. Migration from rural villages, in contrast with the past, is more actively and commonly practiced. The regularization of migrant labor has actually thrown some light on the economic situation in rural villages. It has brought about such positive effects as an increase in cash income, a variety of consumer goods, and an improvement in the household economy. In addition, the consciousness of the people responds to these changes in economic improvement. As for the urban areas and the border areas, a system to take care of remittances has been established and agencies for these remittances have been newly opened.

Following the regularization of migrant labor, the mobility of people has increased, and it makes it more difficult to distinguish innocuous transactions from human trafficking. As the market economy expands, featuring a push dynamic and a pull dynamic, heteronomy and autonomy exert reciprocal influences on each other in complicated ways. Under these circumstances, migratory workers still remain vulnerable to the exploitation of human trafficking. At present, migrant labor in itself is commonly practiced around the globe. However, there are still more problems regarding safer migration to be dealt with. In this regard, it is important to pay close attention to the actual situation of migratory workers so as not to minimize the problems. Usually, when they decide to migrate, workers depend on a human network, which is a closely connected group of people, for example, their family members or relations. In fact, it is the poor and needy family which falls back on brokers to find employment. This situation endures. Generally speaking, a broker appears in a rural village and makes up a story of a "dream migration," deliberately showing a "classic example of successful migration" to lure a needy person into human trafficking. As mentioned earlier in the text, people who decided to migrate were swallowed up by an exploitative structure of human trafficking without being aware of what was happening. Once they were trapped into human trafficking, they had to go through the process of its victimization. There is still no end to such cases.

In analyzing the Cambodian situation of human trafficking, it is effective to employ the theory which interprets poverty as the deprivation of capabilities. From a structural point of view, it is important to grasp the influence of structural violence on the needy. This book attempts to illustrate occasions where vulnerable individuals achieved their own independence by developing a sense of self-awareness and self-direction. It also showed occasions where they took the first step forward to respond to the change of the social system. Even though they are still exposed to structural violence, they can be confident in themselves by building good relationships with peer supporters.

An attempt to improve the existing social structure, at first, calls for restoring a sense of self-direction in the minds of the vulnerable because they are made to be passive, and sometimes treated as mere objects. Second, it is necessary for them to cultivate independence of mind. Finally, it is essential to build the right balance between peaceful coexistence and individual independence in society. From these points of view, we need to look at the existing society again more carefully.

This social reconstruction is to be started with the intervention of appropriate supporting organizations. With the help of external support, the vulnerable learn to develop a sense of help in order to be liberated from the poverty trap. When they understand the meaning of social power, the vulnerable develop sympathy toward other vulnerable people. Out of genuine sympathy, they set out to build a network with the intention of supporting each other. When the vulnerable are closely joined with each other, the sense of unity shared between them brings about a driving force to change the existing social environment for the better. Eventually, it leads to restoring the human rights of the vulnerable and to protecting them from infringements against their humanity.

Strictly speaking, to bring about social improvement requires the vulnerable to have the right to achieve well-being. In the hierarchal society, they are marginalized and denied opportunities in life on the grounds of their poverty. If poverty is a product of the present social relations, poverty can be reduced by replacing rigidity with leniency in the social relations. It is actualized after people around the vulnerable try to gain a deep awareness of the suffering of the economically underprivileged, by looking at them in a different light. When the social conditions improve, the right to achieve well-being and the opportunity to realize self-fulfillment opens up before them.

It is essential for the vulnerable to develop a sense of self-direction. Accordingly, they need to have confidence in themselves through social participation. People around them can lend a hand to encourage them to become aware of the importance of the expansion of their capabilities. They can also work together with them on their problems. Meaningful relations between them and other members of society depend on empowering and caring. Nonetheless, when these vulnerable women start to lead their lives by taking the initiative, obstacles abound. The hardship they will encounter is far beyond all imagination.

Although they still carry the scars left by their suffering in the past, these trafficked victims have now made a fresh start and live in the immediate present to the best of their ability. These are the women and girls who were once victimized by human trafficking nearly a decade ago. I would like the reader to think of the reality lying before them: how hard it is for once-trafficked women to live somewhere in Cambodia, and how much suffering they have to go through on the way to their independence. Today is the time when human trafficking is so subtly conducted that it is almost impenetrable. In this situation, the cases of these women victims are not just past history but relevant in the immediate present. The experiences of these victims and their fight for a life with human dignity are worthy of discussion even today. The author would like to mention yet again that it is essential to consider the issue of trafficked women and girls as an existing social problem, not one that is finished.

Afterword

This book was written on the basis of my doctoral dissertation at the Graduate School of Asia Pacific Studies, Waseda University. As a researcher on human trafficking, I have tried to do what I can do for the situation in Cambodia, in return for the resources I have had from my research in the country. However, a researcher is an outsider, and not someone directly involved. I still struggle for an answer to the question, "How could I offer support to the trafficked victims whom I talked to personally?" Even though there is little I can do, my role as researcher is to show the world and society the trafficked victims who have been introduced to me. Thereby, I hope that it will encourage the reader to be a little more careful about the reality which lies before the vulnerable. We also need to pay attention to the poverty and social structures prevalent in today's international society. These perspectives should lead to a reconsideration of the existing methods of aid and support on international assistance.

This book deals with the subject of human trafficking, particularly focusing on women and girls in Cambodia. In actuality, human trafficking victimizes men and boys in Cambodia as well. The situation is more severe for them than ever before. The problem with human trafficking will remain obscure unless we try to bring it to light. Each of us has to offer a steady gaze at the situation and think critically about what can be done about it. I sincerely hope that this book will help the reader to gain a better understanding of the circumstances under which the vulnerable are forced into becoming victims of human trafficking.

At the moment, behind the massive development of cities, many people are left in poverty. The vulnerable are excluded and are relegated to a corner of society. At this moment, behind the discrimination and prejudice against those who suffer from a lack of money, human trafficking occurs and always someone is victimized. Those who were caught up in human trafficking through no fault of their own will have to carry the burden of their experience for the rest of their lives.

It could be said that we also are involved in forming a hierarchal society in which indirect violence remains. If we are party to forming and maintaining a social structure, we must review it. In other words, we should be more careful about a social structure which encourages the creation of socially vulnerable individuals and subjects them to indirect violence. The reorganization of such a social structure has to begin with this critical attitude.

Thinking of the responsibility shared by all members of the existing society, the problems of "Som" and the other women who appeared in the text cannot be understood as just "someone else's business." I would sincerely like the reader not to understand this as just the affairs of other people but to show your concern for them. In my opinion, sympathy toward these vulnerable people lays the foundation for respecting their human rights, as well as their lives. When we appreciate the significance of treating them as deserving of equality in terms of human rights and take action to ensure this, I believe that we can contribute, not a little, to making our society more peaceful.

Appendix

Protocol to Prevent, Suppress and Punish Trafficking in Persons Especially Women and Children, supplementing the United Nations Convention against Transnational Organized Crime

Adopted and opened for signature, ratification, and accession by General Assembly resolution
55/25 of November 15, 2000

PREAMBLE

The States Parties to this Protocol,

Declaring that effective action to prevent and combat trafficking in persons, especially women and children, requires a comprehensive international approach in the countries of origin, transit, and destination that includes measures to prevent such trafficking, to punish the traffickers and to protect the victims of such trafficking, including by protecting their internationally recognized human rights,

Taking into account the fact that despite the existence of a variety of international instruments containing rules and practical measures to combat the exploitation of persons, especially women and children, there is no universal instrument that addresses all aspects of trafficking in persons,

Concerned that, in the absence of such an instrument, persons who are vulnerable to trafficking will not be sufficiently protected,

Recalling General Assembly resolution 53/111 of December 9, 1998, in which the Assembly decided to establish an open-ended intergovernmental ad hoc committee for the purpose of elaborating a comprehensive international convention against transnational organized crime and of discussing the elaboration of, inter alia, an international instrument addressing trafficking in women and children,

Convinced that supplementing the UN Convention against Transnational Organized Crime with an international instrument for the prevention, suppression, and punishment of trafficking in Have agreed as follows:

I. GENERAL PROVISIONS

Article 1

Relation with the United Nations Convention against Transnational Organized Crime

1. This Protocol supplements the United Nations Convention against Transnational Organized Crime. It shall be interpreted together with the Convention.
2. The provisions of the Convention shall apply, mutatis mutandis, to this Protocol unless otherwise provided herein.
3. The offences established in accordance with article 5 of this Protocol shall be regarded as offences established in accordance with the Convention.

Article 2

Statement of purpose
The purposes of this Protocol are:

(a) To prevent and combat trafficking in persons, paying particular attention to women and children;
(b) To protect and assist the victims of such trafficking, with full respect for their human rights; and
(c) To promote cooperation among States Parties in order to meet those objectives.

Article 3

Use of terms
For the purposes of this Protocol:

(a) "Trafficking in persons" shall mean the recruitment, transportation, transfer, harboring or receipt of persons, by means of the threat or use of force or other forms of coercion, of abduction, of fraud, of deception, of the abuse of power or of a position of vulnerability, or of the giving or receiving of payments or benefits to achieve the consent of a person having control over another person, for the purpose of exploitation. Exploitation shall include, at a minimum, the exploitation of the prostitution of others or other forms of sexual exploitation, forced labor or services, slavery, or practices similar to slavery, servitude, or the removal of organs;

(b) The consent of a victim of trafficking in persons to the intended exploitation set forth in subparagraph

(a) of this article shall be irrelevant where any of the means set forth in subparagraph (a) have been used;

(c) The recruitment, transportation, transfer, harboring, or receipt of a child for the purpose of exploitation shall be considered "trafficking in persons" even if this does not involve any of the means set forth in subparagraph (a) of this article;

(d) "Child" shall mean any person under eighteen years of age.

Article 4

Scope of application
This Protocol shall apply, except as otherwise stated herein, to the prevention, investigation, and prosecution of the offences established in accordance with article 5 of this Protocol, where those offences are transnational in nature and involve an organized criminal group, as well as to the protection of victims of such offences.

Article 5

Criminalization

1. Each State Party shall adopt such legislative and other measures as may be necessary to establish as criminal offences the conduct set forth in article 3 of this Protocol, when committed intentionally.
2. Each State Party shall also adopt such legislative and other measures as may be necessary to establish as criminal offences:
   (a) Subject to the basic concepts of its legal system, attempting to commit an offence established in accordance with paragraph 1 of this article;
   (b) Participating as an accomplice in an offence established in accordance with paragraph 1 of this article; and
   (c) Organizing or directing other persons to commit an offence established in accordance with paragraph 1 of this article.

II. PROTECTION OF VICTIMS OF
TRAFFICKING IN PERSONS

Article 6

Assistance to and protection of victims of trafficking in persons

1. In appropriate cases and to the extent possible under its domestic law, each State Party shall protect the privacy and identity of victims of trafficking in persons, including, inter alia, by making legal proceedings relating to such trafficking confidential.
2. Each State Party shall ensure that its domestic legal or administrative system contains measures that provide to victims of trafficking in persons, in appropriate cases:
   (a) Information on relevant court and administrative proceedings;
   (b) Assistance to enable their views and concerns to be presented and considered at appropriate stages of criminal proceedings against offenders, in a manner not prejudicial to the rights of the defense.
3. Each State Party shall consider implementing measures to provide for the physical, psychological, and social recovery of victims of trafficking in persons, including, in appropriate cases, cooperation with nongovernmental organizations, other relevant organizations, and other elements of civil society, and, in particular, the provision of the following:
   (a) Appropriate housing
   (b) Counseling and information, in particular, as regards their legal rights, in a language that the victims of trafficking in persons can understand
   (c) Medical, psychological, and material assistance
   (d) Employment, educational, and training opportunities
4. Each State Party shall take into account, in applying the provisions of this article, the age, gender and special needs of victims of trafficking in persons, in particular, the special needs of children, including appropriate housing, education, and care.
5. Each State Party shall endeavor to provide for the physical safety of victims of trafficking in persons while they are within its territory.
6. Each State Party shall ensure that its domestic legal system contains measures that offer victims of trafficking in persons the possibility of obtaining compensation for damage suffered.

Article 7

Status of victims of trafficking in persons in receiving States

1. In addition to taking measures pursuant to article 6 of this Protocol, each State Party shall consider adopting legislative or other appropriate measures that permit victims of trafficking in persons to remain in its territory, temporarily or permanently, in appropriate cases.
2. In implementing the provision contained in paragraph 1 of this article, each State Party shall give appropriate consideration to humanitarian and compassionate factors.

Article 8

Repatriation of victims of trafficking in persons

1. The State Party of which a victim of trafficking in persons is a national or in which the person had the right of permanent residence at the time of entry into the territory of the receiving State Party shall facilitate and accept, with due regard for the safety of that person, the return of that person without undue or unreasonable delay.
2. When a State Party returns a victim of trafficking in persons to a State Party of which that person is a national or in which he or she had, at the time of entry into the territory of the receiving State Party, the right of permanent residence, such return shall be with due regard for the safety of that person and for the status of any legal proceedings related to the fact that the person is a victim of trafficking and shall preferably be voluntary.
3. At the request of a receiving State Party, a requested State Party shall, without undue or unreasonable delay, verify whether a person who is a victim of trafficking in persons is its national or had the right of permanent residence in its territory at the time of entry into the territory of the receiving State Party.
4. In order to facilitate the return of a victim of trafficking in persons who are without proper documentation, the State Party of which that person is a national or in which he or she had the right of permanent residence at the time of entry into the territory of the receiving State Party shall agree to issue, at the request of the receiving State Party, such travel documents or other authorization as may be necessary to enable the person to travel to and reenter its territory.
5. This article shall be without prejudice to any right afforded to victims of trafficking in persons by any domestic law of the receiving State Party.
6. This article shall be without prejudice to any applicable bilateral or multilateral agreement or arrangement that governs, in whole or in part, the return of victims of trafficking in persons.

III. PREVENTION, COOPERATION, AND OTHER MEASURES

Article 9

Prevention of trafficking in persons

1. States Parties shall establish comprehensive policies, programs, and other measures:
   (a) To prevent and combat trafficking in persons.
   (b) To protect victims of trafficking in persons, especially women and children, from revictimization.
2. States Parties shall endeavor to undertake measures such as research, information and mass media campaigns, and social and economic initiatives to prevent and combat trafficking in persons.
3. Policies, programs, and other measures established in accordance with this article shall, as appropriate, include cooperation with nongovernmental organizations, other relevant organizations, and other elements of civil society.
4. States Parties shall take or strengthen measures, including through bilateral or multilateral cooperation, to alleviate the factors that make persons, especially women and children, vulnerable to trafficking, such as poverty, underdevelopment, and lack of equal opportunity.
5. States Parties shall adopt or strengthen legislative or other measures, such as educational, social, or cultural measures, including through bilateral and multilateral cooperation, to discourage the demand that fosters all forms of exploitation of persons, especially women and children that leads to trafficking.

Article 10

Information exchange and training

1. Law enforcement, immigration, or other relevant authorities of States Parties shall, as appropriate, cooperate with one another by exchanging information, in accordance with their domestic law, to enable them to determine:
   (a) Whether individuals crossing or attempting to cross an international border with travel documents belonging to other persons or without travel documents are perpetrators or victims of trafficking in persons.
   (b) The types of travel document that individuals have used or attempted to use to cross an international border for the purpose of trafficking in persons.

(c) The means and methods used by organized criminal groups for the purpose of trafficking in persons, including the recruitment and transportation of victims, routes, and links between and among individuals and groups engaged in such trafficking, and possible measures for detecting them.

2. States Parties shall provide or strengthen training for law enforcement, immigration, and other relevant officials in the prevention of trafficking in persons. The training should focus on methods used in preventing such trafficking, prosecuting the traffickers, and protecting the rights of the victims, including protecting the victims from the traffickers. The training should also take into account the need to consider human rights and child- and gender-sensitive issues, and it should encourage cooperation with nongovernmental organizations, other relevant organizations, and other elements of civil society.

3. A State Party that receives information shall comply with any request by the State Party that transmitted the information that places restrictions on its use.

Article 11

Border measures

1. Without prejudice to international commitments in relation to the free movement of people, States Parties shall strengthen, to the extent possible, such border controls as may be necessary to prevent and detect trafficking in persons.

2. Each State Party shall adopt legislative or other appropriate measures to prevent, to the extent possible, means of transport operated by commercial carriers from being used in the commission of offences established in accordance with article 5 of this Protocol.

3. Where appropriate, and without prejudice to applicable international conventions, such measures shall include establishing the obligation of commercial carriers, including any transportation company or the owner or operator of any means of transport, to ascertain that all passengers are in possession of the travel documents required for entry into the receiving State.

4. Each State Party shall take the necessary measures, in accordance with its domestic law, to provide for sanctions in cases of violation of the obligation set forth in paragraph 3 of this article.

5. Each State Party shall consider taking measures that permit, in accordance with its domestic law, the denial of entry or revocation of visas of

persons implicated in the commission of offences established in accordance with this Protocol.

6. Without prejudice to article 27 of the Convention, States Parties shall consider strengthening cooperation among border control agencies by, inter alia, establishing and maintaining direct channels of communication.

Article 12

Security and control of documents
Each State Party shall take such measures as may be necessary, within available means:

(a) To ensure that travel or identity documents issued by it are of such quality that they cannot easily be misused and cannot readily be falsified or unlawfully altered, replicated, or issued; and

(b) To ensure the integrity and security of travel or identity documents issued by or on behalf of the State Party and to prevent their unlawful creation, issuance, and use.

Article 13

Legitimacy and validity of documents
At the request of another State Party, a State Party shall, in accordance with its domestic law, verify within a reasonable time the legitimacy and validity of travel or identity documents issued or purported to have been issued in its name and suspected of being used for trafficking in persons.

IV. FINAL PROVISIONS

Article 14

Saving clause

1. Nothing in this Protocol shall affect the rights, obligations, and responsibilities of States and individuals under international law, including international humanitarian law and international human rights law and, in particular, where applicable, the 1951 Convention and the 1967 Protocol relating to the status of refugees and the principle of non-refoulement as contained therein.

2. The measures set forth in this Protocol shall be interpreted and applied in a way that is not discriminatory to persons on the ground that they are victims of trafficking in persons. The interpretation and application of

those measures shall be consistent with internationally recognized principles of nondiscrimination.

Article 15

Settlement of disputes

1. States Parties shall endeavor to settle disputes concerning the interpretation or application of this Protocol through negotiation.
2. Any dispute between two or more States Parties concerning the interpretation or application of this Protocol that cannot be settled through negotiation within a reasonable time shall, at the request of one of those States Parties, be submitted to arbitration. If, six months after the date of the request for arbitration, those States Parties are unable to agree on the organization of the arbitration, any one of those States Parties may refer the dispute to the International Court of Justice by request in accordance with the Statute of the Court.
3. Each State Party may, at the time of signature, ratification, acceptance, or approval of or accession to this Protocol, declare that it does not consider itself bound by paragraph 2 of this article. The other States Parties shall not be bound by paragraph 2 of this article with respect to any State Party that has made such a reservation.
4. Any State Party that has made a reservation in accordance with paragraph 3 of this article may at any time withdraw that reservation by notification to the secretary general of the United Nations.

Article 16

Signature, ratification, acceptance, approval, and accession

1. This Protocol shall be open to all States for signature from December 12 to 15, 2000, in Palermo, Italy, and thereafter at UN Headquarters in New York until December 12, 2002.
2. This Protocol shall also be open for signature by regional economic integration organizations provided that at least one member state of such organization has signed this Protocol in accordance with paragraph 1 of this article.
3. This Protocol is subject to ratification, acceptance, or approval. Instruments of ratification, acceptance, or approval shall be deposited with the secretary general of the United Nations. A regional economic integration organization may deposit its instrument of ratification, acceptance, or approval if at least one of its member states has done likewise. In that instrument of ratification, acceptance, or approval, such organization

shall declare the extent of its competence with respect to the matters governed by this Protocol. Such organization shall also inform the depositary of any relevant modification in the extent of its competence.

4. This Protocol is open for accession by any state or any regional economic integration organization of which at least one member state is a Party to this Protocol. Instruments of accession shall be deposited with the secretary general of the United Nations. At the time of its accession, a regional economic integration organization shall declare the extent of its competence with respect to matters governed by this Protocol. Such organization shall also inform the depositary of any relevant modification in the extent of its competence.

Article 17

Entry into force

1. This Protocol shall enter into force on the ninetieth day after the date of deposit of the fortieth instrument of ratification, acceptance, approval or accession, except that it shall not enter into force before the entry into force of the Convention. For the purpose of this paragraph, any instrument deposited by a regional economic integration organization shall not be counted as additional to those deposited by member states of such organization.

2. For each state or regional economic integration organization ratifying, accepting, approving, or acceding to this Protocol after the deposit of the fortieth instrument of such action, this Protocol shall enter into force on the thirtieth day after the date of deposit by such state or organization of the relevant instrument or on the date this Protocol enters into force pursuant to paragraph 1 of this article, whichever is the later.

Article 18

Amendment

1. After the expiry of five years from the entry into force of this Protocol, a State Party to the Protocol may propose an amendment and file it with the secretary general of the United Nations, who shall thereupon communicate the proposed amendment to the States Parties and to the Conference of the Parties to the Convention for the purpose of considering and deciding on the proposal. The States Parties to this Protocol meeting at the Conference of the Parties shall make every effort to achieve consensus on each amendment. If all efforts at consensus have been exhausted and no

agreement has been reached, the amendment shall, as a last resort, require for its adoption a two-thirds majority vote of the States Parties to this Protocol present and voting at the meeting of the Conference of the Parties.

2. Regional economic integration organizations, in matters within their competence, shall exercise their right to vote under this article with a number of votes equal to the number of their member states that are Parties to this Protocol. Such organizations shall not exercise their right to vote if their member states exercise theirs and vice versa.

3. An amendment adopted in accordance with paragraph 1 of this article is subject to ratification, acceptance, or approval by States Parties.

4. An amendment adopted in accordance with paragraph 1 of this article shall enter into force in respect of a State Party ninety days after the date of the deposit with the secretary general of the United Nations of an instrument of ratification, acceptance, or approval of such amendment.

5. When an amendment enters into force, it shall be binding on those States Parties which have expressed their consent to be bound by it. Other States Parties shall still be bound by the provisions of this Protocol and any earlier amendments that they have ratified, accepted, or approved.

Article 19

Denunciation

1. A State Party may denounce this Protocol by written notification to the secretary general of the United Nations. Such denunciation shall become effective one year after the date of receipt of the notification by the secretary general.

2. A regional economic integration organization shall cease to be a Party to this Protocol when all of its member states have denounced it.

Article 20

Depositary and languages

1. The secretary general of the United Nations is designated depositary of this Protocol.

2. The original of this Protocol, of which the Arabic, Chinese, English, French, Russian, and Spanish texts are equally authentic, shall be deposited with the secretary general of the United Nations.

In witness whereof, the undersigned plenipotentiaries, being duly authorized thereto by their respective governments, have signed this Protocol.

Bibliography

Amakawa, Naoko, ed. *Kanbojia no fukko kaihatsu* [Reconstruction and Development in Cambodia]. Chiba: The Institute of Developing Economies, 2001.

——, ed. *Asean kameika no kanbojia: syakai keizai no genjyo* [Cambodia as a Member State of ASEAN: the Actual State of Socio-Economics]. Chiba: The Institute of Developing Economies, 2003.

Amer, Ramses. "The Ethnic Vietnamese in Cambodia: A Minority at Risk?" From *Contemporary Southeast Asia*, Vol. 16, No. 2, September 1994. In *Cambodia: Change and Continuity in Contemporary Politics*, edited by Sorpong Peou, 445–475. Routledge Revivals. London: Routledge, 2001.

ADHOC (Cambodian Human Rights and Development Association). *RAPE: Attitudes and Solutions in Cambodia*. Phnom Penh: ADHOC, 2004.

Asia Development Bank (ADB). *Cambodia Country Report: Capacity Building for Resettlement Risk Management – Regional and Sustainable Development Department*. Manila: ADB, 2007.

ADB. *Review of Configuration of the Greater Mekong Sub-Region Economic Corridors*, 2016. Accessed November 15, 2018. http://documents1.worldbank.or g/curated/en/580101540583913800/pdf/127247-REVISED-CambodiaUrbanizatio nReportEnfinal.pdf.

Asia Foundation. *The Review of a Decade of Research on Trafficking in Persons*. Phnom Penh: The Asia Foundation, 2006.

Bales, Kevin. *Disposable People: New Slavery in the Global Economy*. Berkeley, CA: University of California Press, 1999.

Barry, Kathleen. *Female Sexual Slavery*. Englewood Cliffs, NJ: Prentice-Hall, 1979.

Berdal, Mats and Leifer, Michael. "Cambodia." In *The New Interventionism 1991–1994: United Nations Experience in Cambodia, Former Yugoslavia and Somalia*, edited by J. Mayall, 25–58. Cambridge: Cambridge University Press, 1996.

CARE International. *Men are Gold, Women are Cloth*. Phnom Penh: CARE International in Cambodia, 1994.

————. *A Good Wife: Discussions with Married Women about Life, Health, Marriage and Sexuality*. Phnom Penh: CARE International in Cambodia, 2001.

Chandler, David P. *Brother Number One: a Political Biography of Pol Pot*. Boulder, CO: Westview Press, 1999.

————. *A History of Cambodia*. Boulder, CO: Westview Press, 2000.

Coomaraswamy, Radhika and Office of the High Commissioner for Human Rights. *Elimination of Violence against Women*. Commission on Human Rights Resolution 2002/52, E/2002/23-E/CN.4/2002/200, Office of the High Commissioner for Human Rights, United Nations, 2002.

Council for Social Development (CSD). *National Poverty Reduction Strategy 2003–2005*. Phnom Penh: CSD, The Royal Government of Cambodia, 2002.

Counter Trafficking in Persons Project (CTIP II). *Where is the Horizon?: Trafficked on Fishing Vessels*. Phnom Penh: CTIP II, 2014.

Delvert, Jean. *Kambojia no noumin: sizenn: syakai: bunnka, 2002 [Le paysan cambodgien]*. Paris: Mouton, 1961, translated by Yoshiaki Ishizawa and Koukichi Oikawa. Tokyo: Fuukyousya, 2002.

Derks, Annska, Henke, Roger, and Vanna, Ly. *Review of a Decade of Research on Trafficking in Persons*. Phnom Penh: Center for Advanced Study and the Asia Foundation, 2006.

ECPAT-Cambodia. *Database Report – Project on "NGO Joint Statistics on Rape and Trafficking 2003–2004."* Phnom Penh: ECPAT-Cambodia, 2005.

Galtung, Johan. "Peace: Research Education Action; Peace, War, and Defense; Peace and Social Structure; Peace and World Structure; and What Happened and Why?" In *Kouzouteki bouryoku to heiwa* [Structural Violence and Peace], translated by Sakio Takayanagi, Tamotsu Shiotani, and Yumiko Sakai. Tokyo: Chuo University Press, 1991.

Healthcare Center for Children (HCC). *Studies on The Main Locations of Trafficking and Sexual Exploitation of Women and Children between Vietnam, Cambodia and Thailand*. Phnom Penh: HCC, 2002.

Heng, Chammroen and Thida, Khus. Survey *Report on Cross Border Migration and Trafficking Bamteay Mean Chey Province*. Phnom Penh: ILO-IPEC, 2004.

Hugo, Graeme. *Migration in the Asia-Pacific Region, A Paper Prepared for the Policy Analysis and Research Programme of the Global Commission on International Migration*, 2005. Accessed August 15, 2014. https://www.iom.int/jahia/webdav/site/myjahiasite/shared/shared/mainsite/policy_and_research/gcim/rs/RS2.pdf.

Huguet, Jerrold W. and Chamratrithirong, Aphichat, eds. *Migration Report 2011: Migration for Development in Thailand: Overview and Tools for Policymakers*. Bangkok: IOM, 2011.

International Labour Organization (ILO). *The Mekong Challenge Destination Thailand: A Cross-Border Labour Migration Survey in Banteay Meanchey Province*. Cambodia, Bangkok: ILO, 2005.

————. *Forced Labour, Human Trafficking and Slavery, Fact Figures*. Geneva: ILO, 2014.

————. *Cambodian Garment and Footwear Sector Bulletin, Issue 4*. August 2016. Phnom Penh: ILO National Coordinator for Cambodia, 2016.

————. *Global Estimates of Modern Slavery: Forced Labour and Forced Marriage.* Geneva: ILO, 2017.

International Monetary Fund (IMF). *Cambodia: Selected Issues and Statistical Appendix: IMF Country Report 06/265.* June 23, 2006, IMF.

ILO-IPEC. *Labour Migration and Trafficking within the Greater Mekong Sub-Region.* Bangkok: ILO, 2001.

————. *Moving Forward: Secondary Date Review of Sending and Receiving Areas and Employment Sectors in Prevention of Trafficking Children and Women in Cambodia.* Phnom Penh: ILO, 2004.

International Monetary Fund) (IMF). *Cambodia: Statistical Appendix, IMF Country Report No. 04/330,* October. Washington DC: IMF, 2004.

Japan International Cooperation Agency (JICA). *Kanbojia kunibetsu enjo kenkyu-kai: fukkou kara kaihatsu he* [Country Study for Japan's Official Development Assistance to the Kingdom of Cambodia: From Reconstruction to Development]. Tokyo: Japan International Cooperation Agency, 2001.

Kingdom of Cambodia. *Declaration on Measures to be Taken for the Implementation of the National Five Year Plan Against Child Trafficking and Sexual Exploitation 2000–2004.* Royal Government of Cambodia.

————. *The Constitution of Kingdom of Cambodia, 1993.* Accessed 27 January 2020. https://cambodia.ohchr.org/~cambodiaohchr/sites/default/files/Constitution_ENG.pdf.

————. *The Law on Suppression of Human Trafficking and Sexual Exploitation.* https://www.ilo.org/dyn/natlex/docs/ELECTRONIC/93355/109099/F-410631367/KHM93355%20Eng.pdf (Unofficial Translation: 03/03/08 by UNICEF).

————. *Law on Suppression of the Kidnapping, Trafficking and Exploitation of Human Persons,* 1996. Accessed 27 January 2020. https://www.ilo.org/dyn/natlex/docs/ELECTRONIC/59890/60877/F65566.

Ledgerwood, Judy L. "Gender Symbolism and Culture Change: Viewing the Virtuous Woman in the Khmer Story 'Mea Yoeng.'" In *Cambodian Culture Since 1975: Homeland and Exile,* edited by May M. Ebihara, Carol A. Mortland, and Judy Ledgerwood, 119–128. Ithaca, NY: Cornell University Press, 1994.

————. "Politics and Gender: Negotiating Conceptions of the Ideal Woman in Present Day." From *Asia Pacific Viewpoint,* Vol. 37, No. 2, August 1996. In *Cambodia: Change and Continuity in Contemporary Politics,* edited by Sorpong Peou, 409–430. Routledge Revivals. London: Routledge, 2001.

Legal Support for Children and Women (LSCW). *Gender Analysis of the Patterns of Human Trafficking into and through Koh Kong Province.* Phnom Penh: LSCW, 2005.

————. *Needs Assessment and Analysis of the Situation of Cambodian Migration Workers in Klong Yai District Trad, Thailand.* Phnom Penh: LSCW, 2005.

LICADHO (Cambodian League for the Promotion and Defense of Human Rights). *Cambodian Women Report 2004: A Brief on the Situation of Women in Cambodia.* Phnom Penh: LICADHO, 2004.

————. *Rape and Indecent Assault.* Phnom Penh: LICADHO, 2004.

————. *Violence Against Women in Cambodia.* Phnom Penh: LICADHO, 2006.

Ly, Vichuta, ed. *Gender, Human Trafficking, and the Criminal Justice System.* Phnom Penh: Asia Regional Cooperation to Prevent People Trafficking (ARCPPT) and AusAID, 2003.

MacKinnon, Catharine A. *Toward a Feminist Theory of the State.* Cambridge, MA: Harvard University Press, 1989.

Ministry of Education, Youth and Sport. *Education in Cambodia 2000.* Phnom Penh: Ministry of Education, Youth and Sport, 2000.

———. *Education Statistics & Indicators 2015–2016.* Phnom Penh: Department of Education Management Information System (DoEMIS), April 2016.

Ministry of Planning. *Report of Provincial in April 2004.* Phnom Penh: Ministry of Planning, 2004.

———. *National Strategic Development Plan. Royal Government of Cambodia.* Phnom Penh: Ministry of Planning, 2006.

———. *General Population Census of Cambodia 2008.* Phnom Penh: Ministry of Planning, National Institute of Statistics, August 2009.

Ministry of Tourism. *Tourism Statistical Report July 2008.* Phnom Penh: Ministry of Tourism, Statistics and Tourism Information Department, 2008.

Ministry of Women's Affairs (MOWA). *Violence against Women: A Baseline Survey.* Phnom Penh: MOWA, 2005.

Nakanishi, Shouji and Ueno, Chizuko. *Toujisya syuken* [The Sovereignty of the Parties Concerned]. Tokyo: Iwanami Shoten, 2003.

National Institute of Statistics (NIS). *General Population Census of Cambodia 2008 National Report on Final Census Results.* Phnom Penh: Ministry of Planning, 2009.

———. *Economic Census of Cambodia 2011.* Phnom Penh: Ministry of Planning and National Institute of Statistics, 2013.

———. *Cambodia Socio-Economic Survey 2014.* Phnom Penh: Ministry of Planning, October 2015. (Electronic Version) https://www.nis.gov.kh/nis/CSES/Final%20 Report%20CSES%202014.pdf.

National Institute of Statistics (NIS) and Ministry of Planning (MOP). *National Accounts of Cambodia 1993–2005.* Phnom Penh: National Institute of Statistics, 2005.

Nishikawa, Jun. *Ningen no tameno keizaigaku* [Economics for Humans]. Tokyo: Iwanami Shoten, 2000.

Peou, Sorpong, ed. *Cambodia-Change and Continuity in Contemporary Politics.* London and New York, NY: Routledge, Taylor and Francis, 2001.

Roberts, David W. *Political Transition in Cambodia 1991–99 – Power: Elitism and Democracy.* UK: CURZON, 2001, New York, NY: Routledge, 2015.

Sen, Amartya. *Resources, Values and Development.* Cambridge, MA: Harvard University Press, 1984.

———. *Inequality Reexamined.* New York, NY: Oxford University Press, 1992. Reprinted 2009.

———. *Poverty and Famine: An Essay on Entitlement and Deprivation.* Oxford: University Press, 1981, Reprinted 2013. Kindle.

———. *Development as Freedom.* New York, NY: Anchor Books, 1999, Reprinted 2000.

Truong, Thanh-Dam. *Sex, Money and Morality: Prostitution and Tourism in Southeast Asia*. London: Zed Books, 1990.

UNIFEM, The World Bank, ADB, UNDP, and DFID/UK in Cooperation with the Ministry of Women's and Veterans' Affairs. *A Fair Share for Women: Cambodia Gender Assessment*. Phnom Penh: Ministry of Women's and Veterans' Affairs (MoWVA), 2004.

United Nations Children's Fund (UNICEF). *The State of the World's Children 2005*. New York, NY: United Nations, 2004.

———. *The State of the World's Children 2006*. New York, NY: United Nations, 2005.

———. *The State of the World's Children 2007*. New York, NY: United Nations, 2006.

———. *The State of the World's Children 2017*. New York, NY: United Nations, 2017.

———. *The State of the World's Children 2019*. New York, NY: United Nations, 2019.

United Nations, General Assembly Resolution. *The Declaration on the Elimination of Violence against Women*. A/RES/48/104 of December 19, 1993.

United Nations, General Assembly Resolution. *Optional Protocol to the Convention on the Rights of the Child on the Sale of Children, Child Prostitution and Child Pornography*. A/RES/54/263 of May 25, 2000.

United Nations, General Assembly Resolution. *Protocol to Prevent, Suppress and Punish Trafficking in Persons Especially Women and Children, Supplementing the United Nations Convention against Transnational Organized Crime*. 55/25 of November 15, 2000.

United Nations Development Programme (UNDP). *Peace-Building from the Ground-Up: A Case Study of UNDP's CARERE Programme in Cambodia 1991– 2000*. Geneva: UNDP, 2001.

United Nations High Commissioner for Refugees (UNHCR), ed. *Sekai nanmin hakusyo1993* [The State of the World's Refugees 1993]. Tokyo: The Yomiuri Shimbum, 1994.

———, ed. *Sekai nanmin Hakusyo2000* [The State of the World's Refugees 2000]. Tokyo: Jiji Press, 2000.

United Nations Inter-Agency Project on Human Trafficking (UNIAP). *Guide to Ethics and Human Rights in Counter – Trafficking: Ethical standards for Counter Trafficking Research and Programming*. Bangkok: UNIAP, 2008.

———. *Memorandum of Understanding on Cooperation against Trafficking in Persons in the Greater Mekong Sub-Region*. Accessed October 8, 2014. http:// www.no-trafficking.org/reports_docs/commit/commit_eng_mou.pdf.

United Nations Office on Drugs and Crime (UNODC). *Trafficking in Persons: Global Patterns*. Vienna: UNODC, 2006.

———. *Global Report on Trafficking in Persons 2014*. New York, NY: United Nations, 2014.

———. *Global Report on Trafficking in Persons 2018*. New York, NY: United Nations, 2018.

————. *Protocol against the Smuggling of Migrants by Land, Sea and Air, Supplementing the United Nations Convention against Transnational Organized Crime*. New York, NY: United Nations, 2000. https://www.unodc.org/documents/middleeastandnorthafrica/smuggling-migrants/SoM_Protocol_English.pdf.

United Nations, The Supreme National Council with United Nations Transitional Authority in Cambodia (UNTAC). *Provisions Relating to the Judiciary and Criminal Law and Procedure applicable in Cambodia during the Transitional Period, 1992*. Accessed January 27, 2020. https://www.wto.org/english/thewto_e/acc_e/khm_e/WTACCKHM3A3_LEG_11.pdf.

United States Embassy in Cambodia, Economic/Commercial Section. *Economic Significance of the Garment Section in Cambodia*, January 27, 2006.

Vijghen, John L. and Sithon, Khun. *Goods & Girls: Trade Across Borders – Border Research #3 Poipet 2004, Report 58*. April 25, 2005.

World Bank. *Cambodia: Halving Poverty by 2015?: Poverty Assessment 2006*. Washington, DC: World Bank, 2006.

————. *Sharing Growth: Equity and Development in Cambodia, Equity Report 2007*, June 4, 2007, East Asia and the Pacific Region. Phnom Penh: World Bank, 2007.

————. *Poverty Profile and Trend in Cambodia*. Phnom Penh: World Bank, 2009.

World Health Organization (WHO). *WHO Ethnical and Safety Recommendations for Interviewing Trafficked Women*. Geneva: WHO, 2003.

Yagura, Kenjiro. *Kanbojia nouson no hinkon to kakusakakudai* [Poverty of the Cambodian Rural Village and the Poverty Gap]. Kyoto: Showado, 2008.

————. "Kanbojia – tai kottkyo ni okeru keizaikaihatsu no genjyou to kadai" [The Situation of the Economic Development and Challenges in The Cambodian-Thai Borders]. In *Mekon chiiki kottkyo keizaiwo miru* [The Economy of the Mekong Basin], edited by Ishida Masami, 147–180. Chiba: The Institute of Developing Economies, 2010.

Yamada, Miwa. *Tai ni okeru hijyukuren gaikokujin roudousya no ukeireseisaku no genjyo to kadai* [The Actual State of the Receiving Policies of Non-Skilled Foreign Workers in Thailand and Problems], 47–60, in The Global Issues No. 626, November. Tokyo: The Japan Institute of International Affairs, 2013.

Yotsumoto, Kenji. *Kanbojia kenpouron* [A View of the Constitution of Cambodia]. Tokyo: Keiso Shobou, 1999.

————. *Kanbojia ni okeru syakai mondai to hou* [The Law and Social Problems in Cambodia]. In *Kanbojia shi jidai* [Cambodia in a New Era], edited by Naoko Amakawa, 177–222. Chiba: The Institute of Developing Economies, 2004.

Index

ADB. *See* Asian Development Bank (ADB)
aid agencies, 83–84, 92–94
Asia, Southeast, *ix*
Asian Development Bank (ADB), 91
assault and battery, xxiv
authoritarianism, 16, 107

Barry, K., xxvi
begging, 8, 20–21, 24–26, 30–33, 66
border area: aid and support in, 89–95; of Cambodia and Thailand, *19*, 84–85; crossing over, 84–85, 87–89; day wages in, 40n8; migratory workers instructions in, *88*, 97n12; people in line at, *19*; Poipet as, 17–18; protective measures at, 127–28; refugee camps along, 39n2; rural villages compared to, 77–79; vulnerable people in, 28–29
border controls, 84–90
brokers: deception of, 27; dream migration story by, 116; in human trafficking, xx, 12, 25, 35; migration arranged by, 78, 116; rural villages searched by, 27; trafficked victims relationship with, 76–77
brothels: human trafficking to, 3–4, 25; prostitution in, 12, 26; sexual exploitation at, 78–79; in Thailand, 9

Cambodia: anti-human trafficking measures in, 83–87; civil war in, 31, 46, 50–51, 59, 65; currency of, 16nn1–2; day work income in, 21–22; domestic violence in, 73–74; elections in, 45–46; food poverty line in, 82n7; GDP of, 47–48; gender code in, 16n3, 54–56; Gini coefficient in, 53; human rights violations in, 6; human trafficking in, xi, xxii–xxiv, 64, 115; income gap in, 48–49; internal struggles of, 42–46; Japan aid to, 91; Manet's return to, 27; map of, *x*; market economy in, 46–49; mutual support systems in, 38–39; Poipet's workers migration from, 18; poverty index in, 49–50, 81; prejudices in, 5; rural village in, 37–38; SEZ in, 48; 6-3-3 education system in, 56–57; social development in, 90–91; sociocultural structure in, 59; structural violence in, 16; sustainable development in, xv; Thailand's migration from, 88; Thailand's mutual agreement with, xxiii–xxiv; trafficking law in, xxiv–xxvi; UN and situation in, 45; UNTAC in, 46; working permits of, 97n16. *See also* border area

About the Author

Yuko Shimazaki, associate professor of the School of Social Science at Waseda University in Japan, specializes in international development, social development, and in particular, human rights issues. She received her PhD from Waseda University. Since she was an undergraduate student she has been keenly interested in the issue of human trafficking and has spent many years conducting fieldwork in Cambodia. As a researcher, she has rich fieldwork experience in Southasian countries. She has written extensively on the subject in Japanese, but this is her first book in English.

www.ingramcontent.com/pod-product-compliance
Lightning Source LLC
Chambersburg PA
CBHW050607280326
41932CB00016B/2943